# HEART-TO-HEART COMMUNICATION

How to Talk to Your Horse in a New Voice

Teddie Ziegler

**Copyright © 2022** Teddie Ziegler

ISBN: 9-781387-432639

All rights reserved. No part of this book may be reproduced by any mechanical, photographic, or electronic process, or in the form of a phonographic recording; nor may it be stored in a retrieval system, transmitted, or otherwise be copied for public or private use—other than for "fair use" as brief quotations embodied in articles and reviews—without prior written permission of the publisher or author.

This publication is designed to provide accurate and authoritative information regarding the subject matter covered.

**Author:** Teddie Ziegler
**Editor:** Mark Mottershead
**Design and Cover Art:** Jose Pepito, Jr.
**Photos:** Bill Delaney
**Subjects:** Self-Help, Education; Adult education, Instructional, Horses

**Disclaimer:** The author makes no guarantees to the results you'll achieve by reading this book. All horse training requires know-how and persistence. The results and client case studies presented in this book represent results achieved working directly with the author. Your results may vary to these depending on your prior experience and application of the principles outlined.

# CONTENTS

**Dedication** ........................................................................................ v
**Preface** ........................................................................................... vii
    Case Study #1: Pamela and Cody ................................................. xiii
    Case Study #2: Madeleine and Choupette ..................................... xv
    How To Read This Book ............................................................. xviii
    Equipment You Will Need To Complete The Lessons In This Book ............................................................................................. xix
    Your Safety ................................................................................... xix
    Legal Disclaimer ............................................................................ xx
    Your Agreement ............................................................................ xxi
    About Me ...................................................................................... xxi

**Chapter 1**    The 3 Types of Heart-To-Heart Communication ......... 1

**Chapter 2**    Finding Your Center ................................................... 8
    Step #1 - Finding Your Center ........................................................ 9
    Exercise #1 - Hanging Out ............................................................ 12
    Exercise #2 - Be Your Horse ......................................................... 16

**Chapter 3**    Opening Your Heart .................................................. 18
    Step #2 – Open Your Heart ........................................................... 18
    Exercise #3 – Mindful Meditation ................................................. 22

**Chapter 4**    Focusing & Connecting to Your Horse ...................... 26
    Step #3 – Focus and Connect ........................................................ 26

| | |
|---|---|
| Exercise #4 - Describe Your Horse | 28 |
| Exercise #5 - Connection | 30 |
| Results: | 33 |

## Chapter 5   Sending a Message .................................................. 34
Step #4 – Sending a Message ........................................................ 34
Exercise #6 - Magnetic Hands ...................................................... 42
Exercise #7 - Spot Visualization ................................................... 43

## Chapter 6   Listening & Receiving a Message ........................ 47
Step #5 – Receiving Messages (Listening) ................................. 47
Exercise #8 - The Art of Energy ................................................... 51

## Chapter 7   Allowing the Possibilities .................................... 58
Step #6 – Allow, Rinse, and Repeat ............................................. 58

## Chapter 8   Resolving Your Roadblocks ................................ 62
Step #1 Roadblocks ........................................................................ 64
Step #2 Roadblocks ........................................................................ 66
Step #3 Roadblocks ........................................................................ 68
Step #4 Roadblocks ........................................................................ 70
Step #5 Roadblocks ........................................................................ 72

## Chapter 9   The Kind Of Results You Can Expect ............. 75

## Chapter 10   The Missing Ingredient ...................................... 79

## Chapter 11   What To Do Next? ............................................... 84

Dedication .............................................................................................. 89

# DEDICATION

This book is dedicated to my dear friend and mentor "Uncle David" who taught me how to truly listen to nature and love without end.

And to my horse Jazz
who continued to teach me how to communicate heart-to-heart

# PREFACE

*"I truly believe that as children we see humans and animals as the same. We don't differentiate, we're all just beings. And in our innocent wonder, we communicate with animals telepathically without giving it a second thought. We assume it's normal and that everyone can do it, including adults. And then bit by bit, that gift just seems to fade away, and we don't even notice."*
**Teddie Ziegler**

Have you ever watched TV shows about wildlife in Africa? The ones that show the lions on the prowl trying to catch dinner. Have you noticed that the deer or antelope that survive seem to know instantly when the lion is in the area?

They seem to instantly know that there's something different going on, their heads go up and then they start scanning with their ears and noses for confirmation.

Do you know what it is?

It is actually something that is very near and dear to my heart and something I treasure. I know it's the reason horses are drawn to me and

# HEART-TO-HEART COMMUNICATION

trust me, why they come to me for help and why they aren't afraid to be around me.

It is something I've been reluctant to discuss until recently as some people feel it's 'woo-woo' or 'hooey'. And many people are just afraid of anything that's different or strange, anything they can't explain.

However, when a horse senses it in you, he instantly knows everything he needs to know. He knows if you are trustworthy, if you have the right intentions, what your emotional state is, and if you are a threat.

Once he has all that information about you and knows he can trust you, then he will connect and communicate with you on a deeper level. Then all that's left is figuring out how to communicate properly and what the two of you want in order to be happy.

Just like in a marriage. You meet, fall in love, and start learning how to communicate with each other in a way that makes the two of you happy.

I'm sure you've seen people work with horses where it seems as if they are communicating telepathically, it's just so effortless for them.

I've heard people say that this type of communication is unattainable, or only for the most gifted or blessed. I don't believe that is true.

I believe this is a natural ability we all have; we just have to be aware of and be open to learning it.

Some students in my personal coaching program asked how they can also achieve this kind of effortless, telepathic communication and so I began to share it with them.

Now they too can see what I see and do what I do with horses because I have made these skills transferable and teachable. It's been one of the highlights of my life witnessing their transformation into amazing horsemen and women with their own magic.

As I said, I've been reluctant to discuss this for the longest time but have been urged to open up about it by these students.

I call it *"Tapping into the Universal Energy"*.

# PREFACE

Perhaps you are aware of this already, perhaps not. Whichever it is, I have two questions for you…

1. Have you ever gone to someone's house and their cat or dog comes right up to you for scratches, or the cat jumps in your lap for cuddles?

   And their owner says, *"They normally don't act like that with strangers"*.

2. Have people told you that you are good with animals?

If so, then you're already connected to this universal energy. But most people don't realize that they are connected and they're not sure why it happens or how to turn it on or off. They just know that it shows up when they need it.

When you can deliberately tap into this energy and hone this skill, a mere twitch of your head or a shift in your seat is enough for your horse to know exactly what you're asking. And your horse is happily willing to cooperate with you. The two of you will be in perfect sync.

This connection to the universal energy links you and your horse naturally and takes your horsemanship skills to another level.

But it's even more than that though. It's an intuition, a feeling, a knowing, and a deep understanding. A way to communicate with your horse in a deeper, richer, more fulfilling way.

For those people who appear to be able to communicate telepathically with their horse, that could indeed be what they are doing, tapping into this universal energy.

Just as you want to be on the 'same wavelength' in a blissful marriage, the same is possible in your relationship with your horse. And when you are, it allows you to know what's really going on with each other and

# HEART-TO-HEART COMMUNICATION

allows you to feel your way through any issues together. It makes working with your horse so much simpler.

Here's an example of how this worked for me when I was young.

Growing up in the countryside, it was typical to see unwanted dogs dropped off at private schools as people figured that the parents who sent their kids there had the space and means to take care of them. It didn't happen every day or every month, but it was often enough that it was a normal occurrence.

Well, I never met an animal I didn't love or didn't want to help. And every time someone abandoned a dog at my school, it always seemed to find its way to me. I never complained.

Looking back at this, my family and I laugh about it now, but back then I never questioned it. I always felt in my heart that the dogs knew that I could help them so they came right to me. And help them I did.

I would always bring them home with me. I never had to put a leash on them or force them to come home with me. I'd just ask the dog to get on the bus with me and follow me home from the bus stop, or I walked all the way home with the dog by my side.

I never worried that the dog would suddenly run off. I never even thought about it. I just knew that the dog wanted to go home with me.

The dogs could have gone anywhere they wanted, but they never left my side. They knew I would take good care of them and keep them safe.

On one such occasion, I brought home a beautiful golden retriever. She was so sweet and I loved her from the moment I saw her. We walked home together and I just talked about all the fun we were going to have together.

When I got home my mother said, *"It's up to your father if you can keep her."* So I played with the dog until my father got home.

When my father drove into the driveway, I quickly ran into my bedroom with the dog and told the dog to stay there and be quiet until I asked my dad if I could keep her.

# PREFACE

She stayed right there where I left her and she didn't make a sound. I'd left my bedroom door wide open so she could have left at any time, but instead she just stayed there quiet as a mouse.

I ran up to my dad the second he came into the house and said, *"Dad, I found a dog today and brought her home. She's in my room and I really want to keep her, can I?"*

Before my mom could say one word, dad looked down the hallway to my room and the open door and said, *"If you have a dog in there and she is that quiet, then yes, you can keep her."*

He didn't want a dog in the house and thought I was kidding until my mother told him that it wasn't a joke, I really did have a dog in my room. Oops.

When I started jumping up and down excited that I could keep the dog, she came running out of my room, jumping up and down with me. *"We did it! We got dad to say yes!"*, was what I was telling the dog in my head.

Dad then said, *"I thought you were joking. No, you can't have a dog,"* to which my mother said, *"You already told her yes, you can't back out on your promise now."*

My mom made me put up flyers and we even ran an ad in the paper in case anyone was looking for her but no one came to claim her, so she was mine!

I called her Goldie and soon enough she became a part of the family and everyone loved her.

My mom used to laugh at how I never needed a leash and how I talked to her. She could see that the dog actually looked like she was talking back to me. Mom never understood it, but she also never teased me about it. The dog was happy, I was happy.

I think that as we grow older, that natural ability to communicate with our animals wanes and we begin to disconnect from them. The connection doesn't just stop overnight, but it seems to just slowly fade away.

## HEART-TO-HEART COMMUNICATION

During that awkward phase between being a child and being an adult, I think we can still talk with and hear animals, but only some of the time. Those natural abilities somehow seem to become intermittent and uncontrollable.

- Sometimes it's too much, like the volume is turned up too loud, and the animal seems to be screaming in your head.
- Other times you try to talk with an animal and get nothing. Like talking to a brick wall.
- And then sometimes it's like it always was and you can talk with your dog or your horse like it's the most natural thing in the world. And it is.

But then our minds get busy with school, chores, responsibilities, and trying to figure out who we are. Our young minds get filled with lots of new ideas and concepts and what we must do, ought to do, or should do.

Little by little we lose our natural ability to talk with animals as our natural telepathic abilities slowly fade away. The more our brains get full of other stuff, the less we can communicate Heart-to-Heart. We begin to think more and feel less.

I was an introvert as a child and as a young adult so I spent most of my time with animals as opposed to people. Even though my connection and ability to talk with animals became more sporadic as I grew up, it never fully went away.

But I had to learn more about it and how to control my ability. It was natural and innate as a child, but as an adult it fluctuated and I couldn't always control it. However, it was still there deep down inside me somewhere.

That was one of the gifts my dear friend, Uncle David, gave me as an adult. How to tap into this innate ability and be able to tap into it when I wanted to.

I think this innate ability to communicate heart-to-heart is just dormant in most people after they grow up. They just have to learn how to bring it back to the forefront and tap into the energy that allows this to happen naturally between people and animals.

This is why I started my Heart-to-Heart Communication program and wrote this book.

I want to help people tap into their natural abilities to communicate with their horses without words, heart-to-heart.

It has been a blessing to me to be able to do this with my horses. Even my horses love it as they enjoy being heard (no pun intended!) and our relationship is so much better because of it.

Because I know how beautiful and amazing this connection and communication feels, I want to share it and show how I was able to do this and how you can too. My hope is that you will be able to find the same peace and joy with your horses that I found when I could speak with mine.

## Case Study #1: Pamela and Cody

Here's how one of my students realized that it had now become natural for her and her horse to talk with each other.

Pamela was out in the pasture pulling weeds and just hanging out with her horses. She wasn't really paying attention to anything and had naturally gotten into "the zone". She was relaxed, calm, and her mind was quiet and peaceful. She really wasn't thinking about much except pulling the weeds and enjoying the day.

Then Pamela's horse Cody started running towards her in the pasture. She instinctively knew that he was running towards her for help. She could feel his fear and his need for her to help him. He was calling to her, telepathically, as he was running up to her.

A year ago, if Cody ran towards her at full force, as he was doing right

## HEART-TO-HEART COMMUNICATION

now, he would have been attacking her. But this time she knew exactly what he was telling her and she wasn't afraid. She knew this situation was very different.

As Cody got closer to her, she could feel that he wanted her to get the large horsefly off of his rear end as it was biting and hurting him. He ran up to her full force and then stopped right next to her saying, "Get it, get it."

But she couldn't quite reach it so she told Cody, "*Sorry, I can't get it as I can't reach it.*"

She doesn't even remember if she said this out loud or not as she was so connected at that moment.

Cody then told her, "*OK,*" and he turned around as far as he could and lunged at the fly with his mouth. This was enough for the fly to move closer to Pamela so she could get it. She knew without question exactly what he was doing. She could feel Cody's thoughts.

She said, "*Thank you, I can get it now so hold still,*" and Cody stood perfectly still as she got rid of the horsefly and suddenly all was well in Cody's world.

She can't say for sure, but looking back on it, Pamela thinks the whole conversation happened without words. But there was no question that a conversation had taken place.

Pamela couldn't believe it. Without even trying, she and Cody had telepathically communicated with each other. She hadn't had time to stop and think, it just happened.

And it was all so easy, natural and effortless. Their conversation was instinctual. Like it had always been this way and it didn't take any effort or second thoughts.

Pamela and her horse are not only talking to each other without words but Cody is hearing her thoughts, understanding her intentions, trusting her heart, and accepting her guidance. It's a whole new world for both of them and they are doing things together she never thought possible just one year ago.

Being able to talk heart-to-heart with her horse has transformed their relationship, their training, and so much more. She knows when he is hurting, hungry, upset, or sick. And she now knows why because she gets it 'direct from the horse's mouth.'

They have accomplished so much more than before because of the trust, willingness, and cooperation the two of them now share as friends. A true companionship between horse and human.

## Case Study #2: Madeleine and Choupette

If you have read my book *'Herd Bound To You!'* then you will be familiar with how an experienced horsewoman Madeleine had fallen in love with a beautiful Haflinger mare named Choupette.

Having purchased her, Madeleine found out that this spirited little horse did not care for nor want anything to do with humans. In fact, Choupette was super aggressive in every possible way you can imagine.

She was food aggressive, pushy, nippy, anxious, nervous, didn't want to go into her stall, once in she didn't want to come out again, and she bolted in an attempt to escape at every opportunity.

After one and a half years of trying everything she knew, Madeleine called me up and told me that I was her last hope. Otherwise she would be forced to sell Choupette as she saw no future for the two of them despite the fact that she truly loved this little mare.

Anyway, fast forward six months and Madeleine had the horse she had always dreamt Choupette could be.

And if you think this was all down to my hands-on training, you'd be mistaken because this all took place online and over the phone as it was still during the recent pandemic.

# HEART-TO-HEART COMMUNICATION

Choupette is now a totally different horse, very well-mannered, happy, and safe to be around on the ground and in the saddle.

Madeleine was so delighted with the results that we continued to work together and eventually moved on to me teaching her to communicate with Choupette on a heart-to-heart basis.

Here's Madeleine's experience in her own words.

*Last March I started riding Choupette more to help her lose weight and get fit. After one particular ride, I noticed she was breathing quite hard and sweating. So when I tried to tack her up 2 days later, she pulled away and kept backing up.*

*I finally got her inside the round pen and began to ride her. We were doing a nice trot and then suddenly she bucked me off without the slightest warning. I flew over her head and fortunately landed in the snow so no harm was done.*

*It crossed my mind for a moment that perhaps she had reverted back to her old way of being fussy and pushy but then I realized that she was clearly telling me she did not want to be ridden.*

*I hadn't been listening so she must have felt that she had no choice but to yell at me VERY LOUDLY! She was clearly sore and still recovering from our previous rides and was telling me so.*

*This incident opened my eyes to what Teddie had been telling me about listening to my horse and what happens when you go really deep in your relationship.*

# PREFACE

*Since the fall shook me, it took me a little while to get my courage back up to ride Choupette again. But when I went out in the pasture to catch her, she came running up to me.*

*I told her I would like to ride and if she was fine with that, she could come with me. She turned and walked away a few steps. I told her it was completely up to her, she could decide, there'd be no pressure from me.*

*Guess what? She turned around, came back to me and let me halter her. We ended up having a lovely, easy ride together. It was bliss.*

*When it came time to go back in the barn to take off the saddle and tack, she balked at the door. I told her it was OK, we just needed to go inside for a few moments and she could go back outside after. She understood me and immediately followed me in.*

*Recently we moved to a new facility with a nice dome indoor arena. We had never ridden in an indoor arena before so I first let her loose and played with her to make sure she was relaxed.*

*We then started doing some exercises, and to my surprise, she did perfect circles around me at the trot, and on her bad side. I could not believe it. She was so connected to me, it felt wonderful.*

*So I tacked her up and told her if she wanted to be ridden, she should stand nicely at the table so that I could mount her.*

## HEART-TO-HEART COMMUNICATION

*Now bear in mind, she was not always very good at this and often stood at an angle to it which made it tricky for me. But on this occasion she stood right next to the table and perfectly parallel to it to make it easier for me.*

*The ride after was great, again very relaxed, easy and enjoyable for us both. Eventually, she took me to the door to tell me she had enough. I told her OK, I hear you, but let's just practice one more thing and then I would dismount. She happily did that exercise and as promised, I duly dismounted and as I did so she gave me a lovely neigh as if to say, "Thank you."*

Now you may think that this all sounds like coincidence, or that Pamela and Madeleine were just projecting their own desires and wishes on to what happened.

Well, perhaps they did… but what if they didn't?

What if it was truly possible to be so connected with your horse that you can have a conversation with or without words?

True, soul-to-soul, heart-to-heart communication.

Wouldn't it be worth suspending your disbelief and quieting your cynical, adult mind in order to experience it?

Read on and I'll explain not only why it is possible but how you can develop this ability too.

## How To Read This Book

In the Introduction Chapter that follows, I'll describe how I have classified the 3 general types of heart-to-heart communication that I've seen with my horses. This way you can get an idea of what is possible with your horse.

# PREFACE

In Chapter 1 that follows I'll also tell you the steps that I take to communicate with my horses. Which will hopefully help ease your concerns knowing that it can happen just as easily for you too.

We will then get into the nuts and bolts of each step in the following chapters. I suggest you read all the chapters in order without skipping any as they build upon each other. Then go through each lesson and do the exercises within each lesson before moving onto the next chapter.

Sometimes we get in our own way when we try to move ahead too quickly. Reading one lesson, even one week at a time, should help you stay focused and keep you moving forwards.

Please note that throughout the book, I will be referring to the horse's gender as he or him to be consistent. This is primarily because all the horses I have owned in my adult life have been male but if your horse is a mare, please just replace those with she or her.

## Equipment You Will Need To Complete The Lessons In This Book

1. A journal designated specifically for these lessons
2. A pasture or arena to be alone with your horse to practice these lessons

## Your Safety

As always, my primary concern is for the safety and happiness of both you and your horse and I don't want to see anybody get hurt.

Since I'm unable to work with you and your horse in person, you should already have a strong foundation on how to handle your horse from the ground and how to keep yourself safe when around your horse.

You must already have basic horsemanship skills and have the ability

# HEART-TO-HEART COMMUNICATION

to move your horse away from you easily, at any speed. This will protect you in many situations.

I may also advise you sometimes to use a reed or a whip to help you keep your horse at a safe distance. However, please do not take this as a recommendation to hit your horse. I never hit a horse in my care. Rather, these items are for you to use as tools (extensions of your body) to create a larger, protective bubble around yourself.

If the questions being asked of you by your horse are not matched by your experience level or your ability with horses, then I always recommend that you seek outside help from someone more experienced than yourself, rather than going at it alone.

In addition, if you are not achieving the results you want or you sense that there is a chance either you or your horse could get hurt, then stop and seek direct help from a suitably qualified instructor or you can book a consultation with me here:

*https://teddiezieglerhorsemanship.com/book-call/*

Following on from this, we'd better deal with all the necessary legal stuff.

## Legal Disclaimer

Equine training can be a hazardous activity, which may result in serious injury and/or death.

This book provides general information, instructions, and techniques, which may not be suitable for everyone or every horse.

I can therefore make no warranty or representation and assume no liability concerning the validity of any advice, opinion, demonstration, or recommendation expressed within.

You must rely on this material at your own risk.

I am sharing my experiences with you so that they may help you as they have helped me and other students.

Furthermore, I shall have neither liability for, nor responsibility to, any person or entity with respect to any loss or damage caused or alleged to be caused, directly or indirectly, by the information contained within this book.

## Your Agreement

By continuing to retain or read this book, you give your tacit agreement to the above Legal Disclaimer.

Should you not wish to do so, then please write and let me know via my Support Desk (help.teddiezieglerhorsemanship.com) and I will authorize an immediate refund for you.

## About Me

My name is Teddie Ziegler, and like everyone else, I am a blend of my parents in both personality and heritage. Because of that, I feel very blessed. My father was a research psychologist for the government, and I got my love of research from him. He is also a kind and gentle man who is always willing to help anyone in need.

My mother was a social worker with a heart of gold. She always went the extra mile to help someone out, no matter what their situation. My mother is where I get my bleeding heart, my love of animals, and my strong will to help the underdog.

In my case, it has become all about helping give horses a voice. I also enjoy helping their owners understand them better. My goal is to develop the relationship and performance of their dreams for both the human and the horse.

I got my first horse when I was six years old, a little Shetland pony called Farnley's Notable. He came home with me after being abandoned by his owner. He lived in my parents' garage until we could build a barn in our backyard. He was my first rescue horse, but not my last.

Like most horse-crazy little girls, I spent as much time around horses as I could. I competed in many English disciplines. I won ribbons and trophies in jumping, English pleasure, show hunter, and classical dressage. I did this all as a child and as a young adult.

As idyllic as my childhood sounds, it wasn't always like that. I've been through several traumatic experiences which have not only shaped my life but greatly impacted my approach with horses.

I suffered trauma and abuse as both a child and a young adult but my horses (Farnley, Tinkerbell, and Honey) helped me heal through the years. As a result, I have always wanted to give back to horses what they have so graciously provided me: healing, trust, and protection.

To this day, I especially resonate with the plight of rescue horses and I'm sure it's because of the trauma and abuse we both share.

I'm originally from Maryland and went to Towson University after leaving high school, where I earned a bachelor's degree and a master's degree in behavioral psychology.

Family is very important to me and as my parents had decided to retire in California, I moved out there to be with them a few years after graduation.

I worked for one of the nation's leading mental health facilities helping with autistic children and elderly patients, and later became a private therapist for Alzheimer's patients.

My first love though has always been horses and so after studying with some of the top names in the horse industry, I became a trainer myself.

I purchased a quarter horse who had been trained in cutting. This was Jazz. I tried to do English disciplines with him, but he obviously preferred Western, so I went with the flow (HINT: one of my 'secrets')

# PREFACE

and schooled with some wonderful Western-disciplined trainers. Jazz taught me a lot himself as well.

We ended up competing together in Western equitation, Western pleasure, cutting, and team penning. We had a blast and were a really good team together.

I bred Jazz, who sired Apollo, and apart from a brief period (a story for another day), the three of us spent the next 31 years together until Jazz passed away at the age of 34 in 2020. Apollo followed not long after in mid-2021 when he died of a heart attack during a severe tornado that came through the farm. I miss them both to this day.

In 2016 I had acquired another horse, D'Artagnan, who I quickly discovered was my soul horse. So as you can imagine, I was shattered when he unexpectedly passed away from a brain aneurysm in 2020. You can read about it here:

*https://teddiezieglerhorsemanship.com/forever-loving-home-for-horses/*

I have learned so much from these guys over the years, as well as my other three horses growing up. It has truly been an extraordinary privilege to have been in their lives, and I owe them a huge debt of gratitude. They will all hold a special place in my heart forever.

I'm delighted to report though that a new horse entered my life a year ago (at the time of writing) and you can follow Merlin's progress this past year, starting here:

*https://teddiezieglerhorsemanship.com/a-gift-from-jazz/*

Over the years I have taught a lot of courses. I've taught basic horsemanship, safety around horses, relationship and behavioral training, liberty and groundwork. I have also given riding lessons to both adults and children. Yet it has always intrigued me why some people get results

## HEART-TO-HEART COMMUNICATION

while others don't and why some horses react in certain ways and others are completely the opposite.

After a while I started studying equine science and doing research like my father had done. What I discovered surprised me, as it often went against much of what we are taught about horses.

I added these findings to my own personal experiences, my knowledge of behavioral psychology from my university days, and blended all that with my mother's compassionate heart-guided ways to come up with my own unique approach to training horses. This is what lead me to my way of communicating to horses, heart-to-heart. I hope you like it!

I always want to allow horses to have a voice and allow them to take part in the conversation. This has always felt right to me. It was instinctual for me when growing up, and it still feels right today. I even allow my horses to say "no" sometimes instead of always expecting them to do what I say.

Have you ever heard of such heresy?!

The truth is, when you allow your horse to do this, he will thank you for it. And you will suddenly see a noticeable change in his responses and demeanor as the light sparkles in his eyes.

This unique blend of insight, understanding, and empathy has provided me with the tools to create a truly flexible approach, which can easily be modified and adjusted to any situation and any horse.

We are all individuals and so are our horses, and when you take the leap to allow your horse to have his say in your relationship, the connection, communication, and companionship you've always dreamt of become possible.

My burning desire is to help both humans and their horses get to know each other better. By doing this they can become the best possible partners for each other and guarantee that the horse gets the forever-loving home he deserves.

Many people, especially women, naturally resonate with this softer,

# PREFACE

more sympathetic approach. As an example, one student recently wrote this to me:

*"SInce I have been following your courses and learning to 'listen to my horse', we have had some lovely moments of connection that I would never have had if I had stayed on my path of go, go, go. Grab my horse, groom and out for a ride. These days my rides are much more leisurely. Thank you for all your insight, Teddie."*

I've had the privilege and pleasure of helping thousands of students reach success over the past three decades and I have personally worked with over five hundred horses, so you can rest assured what you are about to learn has been thoroughly road-tested.

By learning to listen to what your horse is telling you and responding in kind, this will open up a whole new world of potential for the two of you.

A world where it is indeed possible to communicate with each other with a new voice. Through a deep connection of love and trust, heart-to-heart. By being open to the possibility and choosing to embrace what unfolds will make what seems impossible, possible. And what's more… it's easier than you think.

# THE 3 TYPES OF HEART-TO-HEART COMMUNICATION

*"The ability to communicate with your horse telepathically, heart-to-heart, is so important in many ways. Just imagine the possibilities of what you could accomplish together."*
**Teddie Ziegler**

As an overview I want to go over a few differences that may develop within you after reading this book and practicing the exercises.

Just as people and horses develop differently, your gifts within the field of telepathy may vary as well.

There are generally 3 different types of telepathic communication and knowing what's going on with your horse. Each person will usually be stronger in one type over another. You will also feel more comfortable and confident using one over the other and will feel more drawn to it.

However, this doesn't mean you can't eventually learn how to use all three types. It just takes time and practice. But you should work on the communication type that you are most drawn to initially.

## HEART-TO-HEART COMMUNICATION

**Here are the 3 main types that I've seen:**

## 1. MENTAL

***Thoughts*** - This is when you are both receiving ideas from your horse and sending your thoughts out to our horse. We actually do this all the time without really knowing we are doing it.

These aren't emotions and they aren't pictures. They are somewhere in-between. It's a sense of knowing, you just know what's going on with your horse.

Have you ever noticed that you often seem to know that your horse wants to go out and graze before you actually get to him? Or have you ever felt that you knew that he was hungry or that he wanted to go to the arena to play?

These are thoughts that your horse is sending you and you just know them before even seeing your horse sometimes. However, even though you already know these thoughts, you can second guess how you know them, or even if you truly do know them.

You think, *"That's too easy,"* or *"It must just be a coincidence."*

How about when you want to get your horse onto the trailer to load up so that you can go somewhere fun? Does your horse act as if he 'knows' what you're thinking?

Guess what? He does know because you're sending him your thoughts and he's listening. You're thinking of your horse getting into the trailer and the place you're going to.

However, this type of communication can easily get lost as we humans have so many thoughts spinning round our head at any one time and we usually can't isolate them.

So, more often than not, you can actually confuse your horse with one thought about going out to play, another about maybe loading him into the trailer, and yet another about the hard day you've just had at work or how hungry you are. No wonder, horses sometimes don't understand what we want them to do!

With so many jumbled up thoughts coming so quickly into our heads, your horse will often stop listening to you altogether. He will simply put up a barrier and stop your thoughts from coming into him and stop sending you his thoughts.

## 2. EMOTIONAL

A) *Feelings* - Feeling what they feel. This is usually the first and easiest type of telepathy. When you can feel that there is a problem, or you can feel your horse's resistance, fear, or joy.

I'm sure you have had friends or loved ones that you could feel were in trouble, or who were about to call you. Maybe even picked up the phone knowing who was on the line.

You probably have experienced finishing a loved one's sentences and may have experienced having the same feeling as them at the same time.

When you do this you are tapping into their feelings without knowing it. If you have had this happen to you, you are already communicating telepathically by receiving those feelings.

But to truly communicate this way, you want to start doing this with intention and purpose. You want to tap into these feelings when and where you choose instead of allowing it to just intermittently happen.

B) *Visions* - This happens through pictures and/or images filled with emotions - seeing what they see. These visions can be in the present or from the past. When you receive these pictures, it can help you figure out what your horse is afraid of or what he wants to do.

This type of telepathy is great for figuring out past or present emotional traumas and will help explain why your horse won't do something or go somewhere. It can also help explain when they get frustrated as they can show you a picture of what the problem is.

I think it's easier for horses to show us pictures, but it's sometimes harder for us to show them pictures. It just depends on how your mind works. So this type can be harder for us to hone in on as it's not the normal way most people communicate.

But this gap (pictures vs. words) can be bridged when we start thinking more in pictures. It takes practice, but I find it a much easier way for me to communicate with my horses.

## 3. PHYSICAL

    A) *Touch* - This is where you can tell what is going on with your horse physically. When you touch your horse you are able to know what's going on with him.

For example: When you know your horse is in pain but not sure where. You can touch his body all over slightly and when you get to the area that is injured, you instantly can feel the heat, the pain, and what's going on inside.

Sometimes your touch will trigger other types of telepathy. It could bring about emotions where you can feel the pain your horse is in and visions (pictures) of how the injury happened.

    B) *Physical Sensation* (without touch) - Where you can feel, physically, where your horse is hurt because you feel it in your own body.

# THE 3 TYPES OF HEART-TO-HEART COMMUNICATION

Sometimes you can feel a headache or a stomachache and you were just thinking about your horse. It isn't your headache or your stomachache, it's your horses'.

This works both ways. You can send your horse a physical sensation as well.

For example: If your horse is frightened and reacts physically to a perceived threat, you can raise the feeling of safety and calmness within your own body.

Your horse then receives this as a physical sensation from you which gives him a sense of security and reassures him that he is safe with you. Thereby helping him calm down.

Because telepathy is an intuitive skill, you can choose what you feel most comfortable with and use that as a starting point. Then as you advance you can experiment with the other types and learn to grow those skills as well.

As you develop these different skills, you will often use more than one of these types of telepathic communication at the same time.

At some point, you will get to where you are able to utilize all of them simultaneously to help you know what's really going on with your horse. This will take some time and practice, but it is possible if your desire is sufficiently strong enough.

## How I Communicate

When I decide to communicate 'Heart-to-Heart' these are the steps I take:
Overview of how I talk with my horse:

*Step #1. I calm down, relax, and find my center while spending time with my horse.*

*Step #2. I then go deeper within and open my heart by bringing about a strong feeling of love, a physical feeling of warmth and happiness, and a strong desire to connect with my horse.*

***Step #3.*** *I then change my focus from within myself to my horse and I make a connection, heart-to-heart.*

***Step #4.*** *Then once I feel my horse connecting with me as I open my heart, I am able to ask a question or send a message.*

IMPORTANT: When you learn to communicate heart-to-heart, you will focus less on what you tell your horse and more on what you hear from him.
Overview of how I listen to my horse:

***Step #5.*** *Once I am calm, centered, happy, and I've sent my horse my message through a thought, feeling, or picture, I then quiet my mind again and focus on my horse.*

***Step #6.*** *I then allow whatever my horse wants to send me to come to me without trying to talk back or interpret the thought, feeling, or picture that I'm seeing.*

This takes time, patience, and practice to send and receive one thing at a time and allow it to flow naturally without putting any judgement or thoughts of your own into the mix.

The more you do this, the more you will understand what your horse is telling you and the easier your type of communication will become.

It is important to start out practicing sending one item at a time and listening in stillness even more.

These steps will give you a solid foundation to be able to start hearing and talking to your horse in a telepathic way – truly communicating heart-to-heart.

## THE 3 TYPES OF HEART-TO-HEART COMMUNICATION

I want this to be a great learning experience for you and your horse. If you need some extra help, I am here for you. There are a few different options for personal or semi-private coaching on <u>my website's Learn page</u>. Plus there is a video program that is designed to go along with this book in more detail if you would like a little more help.

## FINDING YOUR CENTER

*"The more you do this, the more you will understand what your horse is telling you and the easier your heart-to-heart communication will become."*
**Teddie Ziegler**

Each of these lessons is designed to correspond with one of the 6 steps that I go through to communicate heart-to-heart with my horses. However, I want this to be a fun and educational book that helps you find your own way to talk with your horse telepathically.

You do you! Take the time you and your horse need to go through these lessons. This works if you do the work. But don't forget to enjoy yourself too.

## Step #1 - Finding Your Center

Because we lead such busy lives as humans we often forget how to "be" with our horses. That is the first thing you need to learn how to do in order to set the stage for communicating heart-to-heart with your horse.

By learning to just be with your horse and become centered, you also are also learning how to listen.

I had a lot of trouble when I first started learning how to get centered because I am a type A personality and it was hard for me to stop doing something.

I had to practice this lesson over and over for about a month or so until I finally was able to find my center and have a quiet mind. So don't get frustrated if it takes you a while too.

There are a few ways to find your center, but what helped me the most was meditation. Actually it was 'mindful meditation'. I'll go into this in more detail later on.

But I will tell you that the same day I was able to find complete stillness…

…was the same day I heard my horse Jazz talk to me.

I was so focused on quieting my mind I forgot everything else and that's when my mind went blank. I felt so peaceful and still. I had never experienced anything like it. It was great.

At that very moment I heard a voice say, *"It's about time. Hi"*. It was so clear and loud I thought someone had come down to the arena. I opened my eyes and looked around and no one was there.

I looked at Jazz thinking, "No, *it couldn't have been him*". For a second I doubted what I heard since it was so clear. And when I looked at Jazz, he looked at me with such an expression of… *"Of course it was me!"*, I just started laughing.

Then I heard him laughing and I started crying. I was so happy that I finally heard him talking to me and that there was no question it was him. Then all I had to do was shut my eyes again and go back to my center and I heard him again.

After that we never stopped talking. And it got easier and quicker to connect and communicate with him each time I practiced.

So I can't tell you loud enough and strong enough how important this one step is to your success in learning this method of communication.

Without being able to find your center, your stillness, and quiet your mind, you won't be able to move forward. And the rest of the steps will not fall into place as you want them to. Keep working on this step until you can quiet your mind.

As humans, we are so used to talking and giving out information that most of us have forgotten how to truly listen. Listening with our minds, our senses, and our hearts. We've lost that extra sensory perception and we listen only with our ears.

Sometimes we do listen with our hearts and we call it a 'gut feeling'. However, many people don't trust or don't follow their gut instincts because they feel as if they can't go against what they see or what they are told.

While you are practicing the lessons in this book I want you to listen with your heart, listen to your gut instincts, and trust to your feelings. Logic takes a back seat for now.

The most critical step to practice developing your heart-to-heart communication is developing your stillness, finding your center, and quieting your mind. Your intuition is the key. Listen to it, allow it to grow and develop naturally. Trust it.

Learning to just 'be' in your own stillness and be calm, relaxed, and have a quiet mind is also critical for both sending and receiving messages. So it will come in handy later as well.

It may take you some time, like it did for me, because your mind might be full of stuff that wants your attention.

But remember, the time you spend with your horse is time you are allowing yourself to only be with him. This is the time you are giving to your horse to focus solely on your horse. So every other person, thing, job, etc. doesn't exist for as long as you are with your horse.

You can think of all that other stuff right after you put your horse away and say good-bye. But for the time that you are taking out of your day to give to your horse, give him your full attention. Everything else goes away temporarily.

**That means no phones as well!**

Have you ever been on a date…

- Where your date is constantly looking at his phone?
- Where your date is watching other people around you and looking right through you?
- Where he is so focused on everything going on around that he's not paying any attention to you?
- Where his focus is so scattered that you don't feel heard or appreciated?

That's a date you never want to repeat, isn't it? I've been on dates like this and never had a second one. If my date can't pay more attention to me than he does other people in the room (aka complete strangers), just for that hour or so, then he's obviously not interested in me.

Well, don't do that to your horse. It makes him feel uncared for, unloved, and unappreciated. Really. You know how sensitive horses are and they do pick up on these things.

You're only there for a small part of your entire day, so be there for your horse. Be there 100%, focused, and interested in him and what you're trying to accomplish together. It makes a difference.

Get yourself in the right frame of mind, find your center so you can be calm, and just 'be' there with your horse. There's a difference between 'being' and 'doing'. You know what I'm talking about.

## HEART-TO-HEART COMMUNICATION

When you focus on centering yourself and concentrate fully, you will be able to find that stillness within you. You will be able to control and shut down the distractions that monopolize your everyday thoughts.

The more you practice, the easier it will become. Then you will notice how natural and simple the entire process is and you will be able to communicate with your horse easily and effortlessly.

You will just need to open the correct line to send and receive communication.

This process alone sounds simpler than it really is. But don't make it too complicated either. With practice it will become very simple.

Here are some exercises to help you find your center:

## Exercise #1 - Hanging Out

All you are going to do in this exercise is literally just hang out with your horse. This requires only common sense in how to keep yourself and your horse safe by picking a safe area to hang out, keeping a safe distance from your horse, and being alert.

The first rule is never to work your horse anywhere where he is not comfortable. So make sure wherever you hang out, it is a place your horse feels comfortable. This can be in a field alone, this can be in his paddock, or this can be in an arena.

Please do not do this in a small stall as that is not safe and your horse is truly not free to move around and leave your area if he wants. You're basically intruding on his space if you try to do this in a small stall or a small round pen.

Make sure your horse is truly free without any tack. You should be hanging out at liberty, which means no halter or anything else on his body. But I do want you to have food and water for your horse wherever you decide to hang out.

After you release your horse in this area, let him run around a bit and allow him to get comfortable before you go in.

Once he has picked 'his spot', then go in and find 'your spot'. Your spot should be away from his spot for now. Not too far and not too close.

You don't want to intrude on 'his safe spot'. And you don't need to be all the way on the other side of the arena either. That will look, from your horse's perspective, like you're trying to avoid him and that you don't want anything to do with him. We don't want that.

I want you to go to your spot, wherever that is, and just stand there for a bit, maybe 3-5 minutes so he knows that you aren't there to make him do anything and you won't intrude on his spot. I want you to just take your time and notice what spot your horse feels is safe.

I also want you to look around and notice if there are any possible dangers. Does the fence look safe, are there any areas that predators could hide, do any trees look like they could fall over, are there any cars or tractors around that could cause him to jump, etc....

Now that you have assessed any possible dangers, you are aware of your surroundings, and you are paying attention… you can walk around a little if you want. You can just stand there in your spot, lean against the fence, or move around the area slowly. Do whatever feels like the right thing to do, but I want you to watch for two things…

1. *Where your feet are, and what's in front of and behind you*
2. *Where your horse is at all times*

So what #1 means is that while you are walking around, look at the ground to make sure you don't step in a hole, that you don't step on a fallen branch that will crack and scare your horse, that you don't trip over your shoelace, or anything else.

Also know where you are placing your feet and that it is safe and you are on solid footing. Also, be attentive to how fast you're moving.

## HEART-TO-HEART COMMUNICATION

If you are walking around, do it slowly and stop and start whenever you feel like it. If you are moving too quickly you may be adding pressure to your horse or telling him to be on alert with your body language. That's the exact opposite of what we are trying to do here.

So just relax and go slowly. If your horse starts to run away or picks his head up high and continually watches you, you know you are going too fast.

If you are just standing or sitting in one spot, just stay quiet and peaceful and observe your horse and what's going on in the environment around you.

What #2 means is that you should always know where your horse is without having to look at him all the time. You should be aware of his breathing, his chewing, the sound of his hooves when he moves, and the speed at which he is going. Use your senses to know where your horse is at all times using sight, smell, and hearing.

Stay clear of his 'safe spot' when you hang out. Make sure to give him the freedom to choose his own special area. Allow him to leave you and be on his own if he chooses. If he comes up to you, let him, but it needs to be his choice.

He needs to know that you don't want anything from him and you don't want him to 'do' anything but be at liberty and free to make his own choices. You are only hanging out together as two individuals sharing the same space.

Your horse needs to learn that your behavior has changed, which shows him that you just want to be with your horse without putting any demands on him. Just like another horse in the herd.

By doing this your horse will start to understand that your thinking is changing and that you are starting to use a new type of language. The two of you are learning something new together and it will take a little practice on both of your parts.

This exercise is not about interacting with your horse, but just being

## FINDING YOUR CENTER

in the same area together doing nothing. Keep it simple, happy and relaxed.

If you can only spend 30 minutes the first time you do this with your horse, that is fine. But if you are like me, that 30 minutes will quickly turn into an hour but feel like 15 minutes! Time goes by so quickly when I am with my horses. Take all the time you want practicing this. You can't do this exercise too much.

Remember: *"The less you do, the more it will happen"*. So interact with your horse as little as possible while practicing this exercise.

When I tell people this, they don't believe me but I can assure you it is absolutely true. Just relax and watch. Every time you do this exercise it will bring you closer and closer to your horse.

Sitting in a chair is actually my preferred method of relaxing and hanging out with my horse. But don't do this until you are sure you are safe sitting in a chair in the pasture or arena with your horse. If you do not feel safe sitting in a chair, keep walking around or standing.

Your safety is the first priority and you need to know how to keep yourself safe while around your horse.

I want to clarify that this and future exercises in this book should be done with only one horse at a time. Just until you have finished the book and have practiced with the one horse. After you have this method of communication down, you can use it with any of your horses.

If you can't hang out alone with your horse, because you are sharing a pasture with someone else's horse, then please take your horse to an area where the two of you can be alone to work on this exercise.

This is a private and sacred relationship that you are working on deepening in order to reach your innate abilities to communicate telepathically. Please treat it as such.

Do this exercise #1 EVERY time you go out to your horse while you are working on finding your center. Sometimes you may want to hang out for just 15 minutes, other times you might want to do it for an hour or longer.

# HEART-TO-HEART COMMUNICATION

But always hang out together for even a short time before you attempt any of the other exercises in this book.

## Exercise #2 - Be Your Horse

Once you are relaxed, you've found your center, and you're enjoying just hanging out with your horse, I want you to go a bit further. Sit in a chair in the pasture or in the arena and continue hanging out a bit longer.

Because now I want you to 'be your horse'. Metaphorically not physically. That does not mean getting on the ground pretending to eat grass like your horse. Do not do that. Remember, you are to keep yourself safe at all times when you are with your horse and that may not be safe.

So after you have sat, or walked around, with your horse in the pasture and you are both relaxed, I want you to use your imagination. I want you to use your visual creativity to picture being your horse.

Imagine what it's like to be your horse, i.e. the same height, weight, age, etc.... I want you to feel what it would be like to have hair, be on four legs, be that size. Use your emotions and feelings and be creative. Picture what that would feel like to you.

Then I want you to imagine what your horse likes to do, where he likes to go, what he likes to eat, and picture yourself doing all those same things. Use your visualizations here and see it in your mind, picture the physical places.

Visualize these things as if you were your horse, not just another horse but your horse. Put yourself in your horse's shoes and see, feel, hear, and picture what it is like to be your horse.

You can do this with your eyes open or shut. Whichever makes it easier for you to visualize.

Have fun with these two exercises and enjoy whatever happens. Just stay positive and don't judge what you do or see, either in yourself or your horse. You can do these two exercises as much as you want.

# FINDING YOUR CENTER

Even though it is important not to have any time demands, expectations or agendas, I do want you to have the intention and the desire to talk with your horse in a new way, without words.

This small shift in behavior will start to change the focus for both you and your horse and open your minds up to something new.

**Results:**

The results that you are looking for from these two exercises are simply to be able to relax, stay calm, and be at peace with yourself while sharing the pasture or arena with your horse. You want to start feeling at ease doing nothing with your horse and enjoying that special time together.

# OPENING YOUR HEART

*"It's the perfect 2-way conversation when both hearts are open. It feels easy and effortless for both horse and owner. But it all starts with a telepathic link that connects you both heart-to-heart, a natural flow."*
**Teddie Ziegler**

### Step #2 – Open Your Heart

When your heart is open and clear, it accepts everything. It holds no judgement or criticism.

I'm sure you've met people that make you feel comfortable right away. You just feel at ease in their presence. People that make you happy just to be around them. Sometimes it even feels as if you have known them for years even though you may have only just met.

These are the people who have an open heart, who are truly interested in knowing who you are. These people are non-judgmental and don't criticize you for being you. These types of people are very easy to be around.

They provide us with a feeling of being in a safe environment, or providing an inviting space to talk, and they do this by opening themselves up to us on a heart-to-heart level.

Because of this feeling of safety, we are more comfortable opening up to them and sharing all of who we are with these people. I'm sure you've met people who you just start telling your life story to because it felt right.

It's the perfect 2-way conversation when both hearts are open. It feels easy and effortless. But it all starts with a telepathic link that connects you both heart-to-heart, mostly without you even knowing it. It's natural. You don't even have to think about it.

When you open your heart in this way to your horse, it allows him to share all of himself with you too. My horses really enjoy our conversations. They like being able to talk with me and that I can hear them. I love it too.

Once you are able to talk with your horse, this type of communication can be used with other animals as well.

<u>Let me share the story of my cat Tiger with you.</u>

Tiger was a wild cat that had been born outside on an abandoned farm that I leased and fixed up when I moved to Maryland from California. The place had been vacated for about 6 years so it was pretty run down.

Most of the first year I never saw Tiger as she was a kitten and had just been born. She had learned from her mother how to hide and survive in the wild. But once I realized there was a small feral cat living on the farm and staying in the barn at night, I started to leave food for her.

She didn't hang around much when us humans were there. And when someone did catch a glimpse of her, she would run and hide from them. She was definitely feral and didn't trust humans. Some people did try to catch her, but she didn't let anyone get within 10 feet of her.

But I knew she was eating because the food was always gone and

## HEART-TO-HEART COMMUNICATION

she looked healthy. So I continued to put it out for her twice a day. Her mother was around as well, but only intermittently.

When it got cold during the first winter, I put out an insulated box with blankets in the barn for her and I put a few heaters around so she could always warm up next to one if she really needed to. The temperatures did get below freezing but she continued to thrive and looked healthy.

I never tried to intrude on her space, force her to come to me, or try to chase her to pet her. I respected her space. Because of this she would come out to greet me every time I drove up but she still kept a safe distance.

After a few months I noticed that when I would go hang out with my horses, she would be somewhere in the distance watching. A few times she would walk along the top of the fence line where I was sitting and just sit for a little while with us.

I guess that as my horses and I were connecting heart-to-heart, she decided to get in on the act too and also connected with me. This became a regular feature of our time together and she started coming closer and closer until one day she came right up to me and allowed me to pet her.

She really enjoyed our connection. It was just as special to her as it was to me.

She was so playful. I was happy that she finally initiated contact and allowed me to pet her. Of course it was always on her terms. But she never let anyone else get close to her. Some of the barn staff tried after seeing her with me, but to no avail. She was still timid with others.

One day a dog got on the property and I saw it from a distance start chasing Tiger across the pasture. I started to run to help her. But then I saw my horse Jazz pin his ears, get in the middle of the two of them and then turn on the dog. Jazz chased the dog out of the pasture in the opposite direction of the cat. Jazz was protecting Tiger.

To my surprise at the time, although not any more, they must have connected heart-to-heart during our sessions too. I was so happy to see Jazz jump in to look after Tiger.

Well, long story short, when the owner sold the property and everyone had to leave, I just couldn't bear the thought of leaving Tiger there to fend for herself again. So, I brought my cat carrier to the barn, placed it on the floor and told Tiger that I really wanted to take her home with me to keep her safe and protect her.

She looked at me with complete understanding on her face and then calmly walked right into the carrier. She then turned around and laid down so I could zip it up. I took her home with me and our relationship since has been even more amazing!

But all that happened because we had connected heart-to-heart while hanging out with my horses. My heart was open to her and there was no question we could clearly talk openly with each other, telepathically. We still do. She is very special.

In order to go to a deeper level of communication, with trust and love, your horse also needs to feel safe with you. Horses need an open heart to connect with, share with, and talk with. Just as Tiger had discovered with me.

> Note:
>
> *When you are extremely depressed, angry, judgmental, or controlling you are closing your heart off to others, including your horse. The more 'crap' you have in your life, especially negative 'stuff', the more closed off your heart is to others. This also makes it very difficult, almost impossible, for your horse to connect with you and talk with you.*

Problems connecting and communicating with your horse are usually because of a blockage in the line. A disconnection. This can be due to a state of desperation, depression, or disbelief. So if something is not working, look within yourself and see how you're feeling.

- Are you too emotional?
- Are you depressed?
- Are you angry or upset?

If you are, then work on those things and just put them away for now. At least put them away for the short time that you are with your horse. He doesn't deserve to feel those emotions with you right now.

Later after the two of you start communicating heart-to-heart, your horse can be your emotional support and your confidant at times. But right now, while you are learning to communicate in a new way, it is too much emotional baggage to attach to your horse. It will slow down or stop your lines of open communication.

This step should be easier than step #1 because you've already found your quiet space and become centered. Now you just go deeper within and open your heart by bringing about a strong feeling of love, a physical feeling of warmth and happiness, and a strong desire to connect with your horse's heart.

Here is an exercise to help you open your heart.

## Exercise #3 – Mindful Meditation

There are so many things you can do while hanging out with your horse, but if you are like me it can be a bit daunting at first. My mind has a tendency to race as I'm usually thinking about 1,000 things at once. So it was difficult for me at first to quiet my mind AND open my heart at the same time.

But you have to have the first in order to have the second. So go ahead and keep doing Exercise #1 and hang out with your horse before you do any of the following exercises.

Start with a quiet mind and become centered. Then move on to this exercise, mindful meditation.

Don't worry, it is not too difficult and you definitely don't have to try to think about NOTHING. In this exercise I am giving you something to think about so your mind can focus on that instead of going back to its normal internal chatter.

I found that when I listened to mindful meditations, not only did they calm me down, but they also helped me focus on one thing at a time. Instead of my mind being like central station at rush hour, it became just about me and the meditation and it made a world of difference for me.

These types of meditations are also very helpful to get you in the right frame of mind to communicate with your horse.

I have meditation audios and videos in my online Heart-to-Heart Communication program but since this is a book, I will give you another way to meditate mindfully. Do this as often as you can to learn to send your horse loving thoughts from your heart to his.

You can also listen to any meditations that you feel will help you become more peaceful and allow you to just 'be' with your horse and open your heart.

**Instructions:**

If you have an audio meditation that you enjoy listening to that makes you feel calm and relaxed, go ahead and use that. The meditation should be something that makes you happy and brings out feelings of joy in your heart.

To start, just sit in a safe area in the pasture or arena with your horse. You can either have your back against the fence so your horse cannot get behind you or be in the center of the area you're sharing.

Place your speaker on the outside of that fence so you can still hear it but your horse cannot get to it. Then, get comfortable, listen, and follow along with the meditation.

That's it. It's easy. So sit back, relax, and enjoy. You can even substitute

## HEART-TO-HEART COMMUNICATION

an audio meditation with some soft music that makes you relaxed and happy. Something that touches your heart.

After doing a mindful meditation like this, most people feel relaxed and calm. They are able to feel a sense of peace within themselves. This is exactly the place and the feeling that you want in order to be able to open your heart and move forward.

The meditation should elicit an emotional, physical, and spiritual joy and happiness within your body and mind.

If you have a happy memory that elicits the same feelings and thoughts above, you can use that instead of this meditation. It could even be a happy memory with your horse.

Just sit quietly watching your horse and taking in the beauty of nature around you and think of those happy memories and allow those feelings of joy to envelope your body and your mind. Be really happy and make the memories heart-felt.

The purpose of using meditations while hanging out with your horse is to help you relax and connect in a deeper way to the heart of your horse. Horses are attracted to safe places, people they feel safe around, calm environments, and happy people.

After doing this Exercise #3, you should practice bringing your emotions into your body, feeling them deeply. Also practice transferring your thoughts into emotions and feelings within your body. Emotions into physical sensations. This will help you in the exercises to come.

Practice feeling the physical sensation of joy, laughter, and happiness within your body. Learn to be content working within yourself. Be happy with where you and your horse are right now. It's a good place to be.

**Results:**

Your goal is to reach a state of complete openness within your own heart.

I understand that this may cause some people to have a moment's pause, especially if they have suffered abuse or other trauma in the past, as happened to me, but please do not worry.

You don't have to open yourself up to the whole world if you don't want to, just open one perfect line of communication with your horse.

And if you are carrying some fear trauma, try to let it go. I guarantee that your heart will be safe and protected when you open it to your horse and it will certainly go a long way to helping you achieve great results while learning and practicing this type of heart-to-heart communication.

# FOCUSING & CONNECTING TO YOUR HORSE

*"Intuitive communication like this is ever growing and changing and that's what makes it so much fun. You have choices and so does your horse. It is special, sacred, and personal between you and your horse."*
**Teddie Ziegler**

## Step #3 – Focus and Connect

So now that you have found your center, are able to bring about a strong, loving feeling within your body and mind, and you've opened up your heart to your horse…now it's time to change your focus.

You were able to focus on yourself and your own feelings in Step #1 and Step #2. Now I want you to focus on your horse and your horse's feelings.

## FOCUSING & CONNECTING TO YOUR HORSE

I want you to focus on your horse in a positive, loving way, without any judgement or criticism.

I want you to be one of those people that your horse prefers to be around and someone he would leave his pasture mates to be with.

<u>Here's a quick story about my dear friend Uncle David that demonstrates how easy and quick it can be once you learn to focus and connect.</u>

First of all let me tell you that Uncle David (David Nuuhiwa Sr.) was a Hawaiian Kahuna, a Lua priest, and he was nominated 'King of Aloha' in 1959, and later 'Ambassador to Hawaii'. He was an accomplished spiritual leader. He was also a dear friend.

He was taught not only to respect all nature but to talk with her, listen to her, and learn from her. He always talked about his teachers – the birds, lizards, fish, trees, water, and wind. And that is what he taught others, how to listen and communicate with nature… the art of communicating through spirit… heart-to-heart.

One time he was on a deep-sea fishing expedition in a boat off Hawaii when the boat navigation stopped working. They were miles from shore and after all the cruising back and forth trying to locate the best fish, no one on board had any idea which direction they should head to get back to port.

So Uncle David sat on the side of the boat and started to meditate. He was actually focusing his energy on the dolphins that were following the boat and connecting with them. He was communicating with these beautiful wild animals.

After a while, he stood up, walked up to the captain and said, *"Follow the dolphins, they will guide us"*.

The captain thought he was nuts, but the dolphins did seem to be just hanging around the boat so he thought he may as well give it a shot. When Uncle David said to the dolphins, *"Okay, take us home"*, the dolphins started swimming. So the captain fired up the engine and followed them.

The captain and other passengers on the boat were amazed when the dolphins took them right to the island they wanted to go to! And after making their usual clicking noises as if to say goodbye, the dolphins just turned around and left. Uncle David then waved and told the dolphins, *"Thank you"*.

Suddenly it became obvious to everyone else on the boat that Uncle David had been communicating with the dolphins. But as always, he just smiled, sat down and waited quietly for the boat to dock.

Uncle David was a very special man.

With time, practice, and patience, that is how easy communicating with your horse can be. So don't over complicate the process that you are now learning. Keep it real and keep it simple.

Here are a few exercises to help you focus and connect.

If you are a visual person, this next exercise will be very easy for you. It will help you focus on your horse and start to connect you at an even deeper level.

This exercise will also help you change the focus from you to your horse.

## Exercise #4 - Describe Your Horse

Go sit in the pasture or arena with your horse again, doing nothing but being with your horse, just as you did in step #1. However, after you are calm and relaxed, I want you to start watching your horse closely.

I actually want you to look at your horse in detail for at least 15 minutes or longer if you can manage it. Ask yourself the questions below and answer them quietly to yourself.

# FOCUSING & CONNECTING TO YOUR HORSE

> <u>Note:</u> *This exercise should be done with only one horse in the pasture or arena.*

**Be very specific!**

- *What color is your horse? Look at every part of him and notice what color each part of your horse's body is and where it changes (if it changes)*
- *How tall is your horse? Is the rear end taller than the shoulders? Where else is there a difference?*
- *How do your horse's feet look? What about his legs? Are there any marks, cuts, swelling? Does your horse favor any leg or limp at all, even the slightest?*
- *How is your horse's mane and tail? Are they thick, thin, short, long, curly, straight? Do they need to be brushed or maintained in any way?*
- *What about your horse's face and ears? What do they look like? Are there any distinguishing markings, cuts, or colors? Do the ears curve in or out? Are the eyes close to each other?*
- *Continue with your own questions as you examine your horse with ever more curious eyes.*

I want you to look at your horse like never before. Examine every inch of him with your eyes, distinguishing each and every individual part from the next. The purpose here is to completely change your focus away from you, to your horse.

Give your horse some food and water if you're working in an arena. This way he will be comfortable and content as you watch him. While you are focusing on your horse, you want to make sure he has something else to focus on.

After you do this, then just relax, close your eyes, and let it go. Let it all go and breathe deeply in and out 3 times and find your center again.

## HEART-TO-HEART COMMUNICATION

Focus on what you're feeling within your body and start feeling what's going on around you in nature again.

This then changes the focus away from your horse and back onto you.

This exercise will teach you how to switch your focus from you to your horse and then back to you when needed. Do this as often as you want in order to help you feel the difference switching focus between you and your horse.

The more you do this exercise the easier it will become.

Well, now that you've learned the foundation of heart-to-heart communication, (relaxing and finding your center, getting in touch with your heart and feeling love, and focusing on your horse) it's time to figure out your preferred method of communication.

### Exercise #5 - Connection

How you connect with your horse is also how you communicate.

Relating to the types of communication in Chapter One, you probably have a better feel now for which one you are already leaning towards.

If you can't recall exactly what the different types are, go back and refresh your memory before continuing so that you have context for what's next.

Is one more pronounced more than the others? Have you been thinking more? Feeling more? Or have you been seeing things in pictures more often?

Once you have this awareness, it will give you a good idea of what to look for when you are connecting to your horse. Knowing what to use when you are connecting, i.e. thoughts (words), feelings, or pictures, will make the process much smoother for you.

It will also show you your preferred method of communication.

## FOCUSING & CONNECTING TO YOUR HORSE

Learning this will help you connect and communicate quickly and it will also help you listen to your horse better.

Of course, your horse has a preferred type of communication as well, but don't worry about that for the time being. That will come soon.

For this exercise I don't want you to try to send any messages, only to practice connecting to your horse and be happy with whatever happens. Don't rush the process.

Be still, comfortable, and at peace with your horse.

To start, go ahead and do Exercise #4 again and describe your horse as I showed you.

However, this time when you are focusing on all the specifics of your horse, start thinking about how you are feeling at the same time. Bring up to the surface your feelings of love when you look at your horse, let yourself go as deep as your heart allows.

Picture your heart full of love and feel that happiness within your body. Be happy and grateful while you are describing your horse. How happy you are that he is the size he is, that he has the beautiful colors he has, that he is so graceful and athletic, or whatever else you love about your horse.

This should connect you and your horse heart-to-heart, emotions to emotions. Enjoy this feeling of connection and love. Smile and be grateful.

You already know that your horse can tell when you're feeling sad, stressed, angry, and nervous, so now lean into the feelings of love, joy, and happiness you feel for your horse because he feels those too.

Once you bring those wonderful feelings out, let them all go and relax again. If you don't yet feel a connection, ask your horse to connect with you. Say a word or a phrase in your mind, or imagine (visualize) the two of you connecting.

Sometimes your horse may not connect with you simply because you never asked. So, ask nicely and politely for a moment or two. If you hear a *"no"* or get a blank wall, just stop and try again later.

## HEART-TO-HEART COMMUNICATION

Sometimes it just isn't a good time to talk and your horse is busy. You have to respect your horse's decision not to talk with you. It could just be a matter of timing.

But if you do connect and you see a picture of something, or you get a feeling in your body, or an emotion, be grateful and just let it go. You may just hear a word or suddenly think a thought, be happy with that too.

After you have finished this exercise, say *"thank you"* to your horse and walk away. Go find a quiet place to be with your own thoughts and write down everything you can remember in your journal.

Just write it down without judgement or trying to interpret it. Then put your journal down and leave it. Go do something fun with your horse like grooming, playing in the arena, or just hanging out again.

Do this exercise over and over but never push it. Just enjoy the process. If you push it or expect too much, then you are going to do the opposite of what you want and you will stop the flow of communication.

Let it all go and be happy with whatever happens when it happens.

For now, you are just cleaning the lines of communication and clearing the way for proper communication. It's like tuning your radio to the right frequency so you can get a clear signal. It takes a few tweaks and turns to get the radio station to come in clearly.

If you have trouble connecting heart-to-heart, remember that this type of communication takes time and practice. Go back and make sure you're centered, relaxed, feeling joy and happiness in your mind and body, and then try again.

It may take a few times. If you start to get frustrated, that will work against you. So if that happens just get up and walk around admiring and appreciating the beauty of nature around you. Once you're relaxed, try again.

## Results:

Your purpose in this lesson is to be open and receptive and to connect with your horse at a deeper level.

You also need to recognize boundaries set by your horse by asking to connect, respecting your horse's space, being grateful, and saying thank you.

By learning to switch your focus back and forth between you and your horse, you will learn to be accountable and responsible for your own feelings. This will help you later on by being able to distinguish your feelings from your horse's.

Trust that what you're seeing or feeling is coming from your horse right now. You will learn discernment later on. Right now, everything is great. No worries and no judgement.

You always want to be gracious and polite to your horse for allowing you into his world, and letting you connect at a deeper level. You want your horse to know that you are happy to connect with him heart-to-heart.

This will also help your sending and receiving skills later on. The purpose of this lesson is to connect only, not to communicate yet. So just go for the feeling of connection with your horse at a heart-to-heart level.

Telepathy is the natural way horses communicate and they are good at it. We aren't, especially at the beginning. So our first baby step is just to connect and be happy.

It's like trying to learn Spanish when our native language is English. We aren't going to be an expert after one or two lessons, but we will learn and grow and become better the more we practice.

# SENDING A MESSAGE

*"Always push the easy button whenever possible. And remember, whether that easy button worked for you or not, it is still a step in the right direction. Even a so-called failure will teach you how to do it better next time. There is always room for improvement and an opportunity to learn something new."*
**Teddie Ziegler**

## Step #4 – Sending a Message

Sending a message is easier than you might think. It's the same as starting a conversation with a friend.

Simply think the thought clearly in your mind without any distractions and send it from your heart. Then be quiet and simply wait for information to come back to you.

The catch is that right now it's like starting a conversation with your friend who only speaks Spanish and you only speak English. But that's just because you are a beginner. However, I want to make it a bit easier for you.

When you first decide you want to send your horse a message you need to do a few things...

I. **The first thing** is that before you send your horse a question or a thought, you need to ask your horse if he is willing to talk with you. It may not be a good time for him as we mentioned earlier. Your horse may not feel like talking right now or may be distracted or busy doing something else.

So, there is no point in trying to start a conversation with your horse if he is not willing to talk with you. Wait until your horse says he's available and then you can initiate a conversation.

You learned how to ask your horse if he is willing and available to talk with you when you were learning how to focus and connect in step #3. So before you try to hold a longer conversation, ask nicely and politely if he is available to talk.

Hopefully you will feel or hear a *"yes"*. Sometimes it is just a physical sensation of a door opening.

II. **The second thing** to do before you start your conversation is to let your horse know you can be trusted and that you only want the best for him. Send your horse the feelings of trust, reassurance, and love directly from your heart.

You can do this while you are hanging out with your horse and combine the two. This should ease any reservations your horse may have about opening up to you.

Use your preferred type of communication with your horse. You can send this initial message in a picture, the thought of safety, or a strong feeling of trust. Keep the feelings, thoughts, and pictures all positive.

III. **The third thing** to do before you start your conversation is to know exactly where you are coming from.

Before sending your horse any messages, you have to feel that strong emotion, feeling, or thought within yourself. This too can be done while you are first hanging out with your horse, focusing on your own emotions.

A simple fleeting thought or feeling isn't strong enough to get through to your horse yet. That is why you should ground the message in a strong emotional feeling or thought.

Once you've practiced this over and over, it will become easier and quicker to talk with your horse and you won't have to go through the process of feeling it within your own body.

But until you can send your message automatically, get used to experiencing the emotion, thought, feeling, or picture within yourself first and then switch your focus to your horse and send him the message with that same emotion, thought, feeling, or picture.

Keep it simple, clear, and concise at first. Then wait patiently for your horse's answer.

Remember not to push yourself, have unrealistic expectations, or be judgemental. And don't forget that after you talk with your horse, you should say *"thank you"* and *"goodbye"*. That's how you end a conversation with your friend, right? So, do the same with your horse.

This is not only showing your horse respect and earning his trust, but you want to disconnect from your horse so he doesn't get constant 'junk mail' from you. When you say goodbye and thank you, you can also send him a picture of a door shutting in order to temporarily disconnect from him.

Once you've had one successful conversation, your horse will know how to connect with you and will be able to send you information whenever he wants. So you may receive messages from your horse without you having to start the conversation. Be open and available for that.

## SENDING A MESSAGE

IV. **The fourth thing** you need to do before you actually send your horse a message is to figure out what you want to tell your horse. Make sure it is clear and concise in your head before you try to send your message.

If you're confused or you change your wording or your thoughts and emotions trying to get out one message, you will confuse your horse. If he's confused he may just end the conversation and walk away.

Get the message straight in your mind **before** trying to send it to your horse.

At first you might try to send too much and this can be confusing to your horse as well. You want your first time to be simple and clear. Don't try to do too much too soon.

To reiterate the steps so far:

1. Hang out and relax with your horse. Get yourself centered.
2. Get the message you want to send your horse clear in your head.
3. Then focus and connect by sending your heart felt love out to your horse in thought and emotion. Feel your love going to your horse and connecting to him.
4. Ask your horse, in your preferred type of communication, if he is available to talk. Asking permission.
5. Ask your question or send your message. Then be quiet and wait patiently for an answer.
6. There is a step 6, listening to your horse's message, but that is in the next part of this book.

Once you have sent your message in your preferred type of communication, you can try sending your message using a different type the next time. Try only one type per session or per day in order to allow your horse to process this. Try what you feel is the easiest for you first.

This way you can practice each type and see what is truly easier for

## HEART-TO-HEART COMMUNICATION

you and what you resonate with more. Plus you may find that your horse prefers one over the other as well.

Repeat these steps and this process every time you want to start a conversation with your horse. Each time allow whatever comes to come and then let it all go again. In and Out. That's it.

It's very important at this stage in communicating that you do not try to interpret anything you receive right now. Just allow it all to flow and happen naturally and by doing this, you will allow more communication to occur. If you start to interpret as you go, you will slow the process down and possibly stop hearing your horse.

Wait until you get better at the communication part before trying to interpret what you hear or see.

Then after your conversation is over, go to your quiet place and write in your journal what happened, what you saw and how you felt.

When you journal, just write whatever comes up for you, or whatever you can recall from the conversation. Again, don't analyze, just write in a stream of consciousness. You can look at it later when you're at home and then try to figure it out.

Eventually you will understand what your horse is trying to tell you and you will understand without having to interpret it. But at this stage use the logical side of your brain to interpret your journaling away from your horse.

Learning how to send your horse messages properly and how to communicate heart-to-heart is more important at this point than what your horse is telling you. I want you to get used to just allowing things in and letting them go for now.

Here are some pointers to remember that will allow your communication to go smoothly:

- Use a strong emotion, thought, or feeling. Try only one type of communication at a time. Not all at once. Remember you are practicing and taking small steps right now.

- Be respectful and polite in your messages to your horse. Keep it positive, simple, and ask nicely.
- Think about how you phrase your question. Instead of demanding an answer or using an interview style, ask in a caring, thoughtful way. *"Can you share with me what you like to eat?"* Instead of *"What do you like to eat?"*
- Be kind and considerate when forming your questions. It will help you receive an answer. Remember these questions and the connection come from your heart not your head.

Horses often send us images representing emotions, thoughts, concepts, or ideas that they want us to understand. Sometimes these are things they want to teach us or show us about ourselves and how they see us.

Last but not least, you can ask your questions out loud if you are more comfortable at first. However, make sure you are still sending the message from your heart and feel it, even if you are vocally saying it at the same time.

I use both ways to talk with my horses and other animals. When I speak vocally I also speak through my heart.

Sometimes it can even be easier to say it out loud while at the same time feeling it because it helps your brain associate the feelings with the words.

<u>Here's a story about how I used this method with a wild baby crow:</u>

I was outside in my driveway one day and I heard this racket. It was a bird yelling and causing a ruckus. I could tell by the noise that the bird was in trouble so I went looking for it.

As soon as I got to the end of my driveway, I saw this baby crow running towards me making all sorts of noise. I quickly realized he was

## HEART-TO-HEART COMMUNICATION

in trouble and needed my help. I could feel the panic in my own body and I could hear him, in my mind, calling out for help.

We connected immediately as he came running to me. I stopped and he came right up to my feet and stood there squawking. In my head, I told him to follow me and I would help him. I turned around and he followed me back up my driveway to the front of my house.

I then turned around and told him that he was safe there for now and I was going to go inside to get him some food and water. I asked him to wait for me. I did this verbally out loud.

I could feel that he was scared, hungry, and hurt. I went inside my house, got some food and water and came back out. There he was, standing right where I had left him.

He had been patiently waiting for me and was now quiet. I could feel that he had calmed down and felt safe.

I sat down on the ground and told him in my mind that it was OK and he was safe with me. He then jumped up on my foot and let me feed him by hand.

He was very young and had probably never been around people before, but he trusted me all the same. He heard me tell him he was safe and he knew that I meant it as I sent him my own feelings of security.

Remember, this baby crow was a wild bird. He wasn't someone's pet bird that had gotten out of the house. His tail was short and seemed to have been chewed up.

The poor little guy couldn't fly and had probably fallen out of his nest for his first flight and then got attacked by a cat.

My next-door neighbor had come out when he heard all the noise and he saw the whole scene.

He told me later that when he first saw me talking to the bird, he thought I'd gone crazy, but was then amazed when the bird started following me.

Then when I told the bird to wait, the neighbor thought for sure that the bird would run off or fly away. He said he could see that the bird actually understood what I said when I asked him to wait.

Then when he saw it jump up on my foot and take food by hand, he thought he was seeing things.

He just couldn't believe that not only did this all actually happen, but he could see that the two of us were having a normal conversation like it was nothing.

He later asked me how I did it and all I could say was, *"I don't know, it just happened"*. The bird needed my help so I helped him.

I named the crow Joe and he stayed with me until he was healed and could fly. I would put him on my shoulder so he could practice taking off and flying. It took him a few goes before he eventually got his flying wings back. Sometimes he used to fly from my shoulder and sit on my head.

When Joe was ready, I let him back into the wild. For a while though, he used to come back every day and say hello. I would make him a bowl of soft scrambled eggs and we would have breakfast together.

Sometimes he would bring me little gifts of gratitude like shiny rocks. One day he brought me a child's pretty pink bracelet. Joe was very considerate and grateful for our connection and our communication.

The next year he came back with his mate to eat. She was more timid but she came with him anyway. Then soon there was a third – a baby. I was very blessed to have them in my life.

If you go onto my YouTube channel you will be able to see videos of Joe and our adventures together. [https://www.youtube.com/@TeddieZieglerHorsemanship](https://www.youtube.com/@TeddieZieglerHorsemanship)

Once you learn how to communicate Heart-to-Heart with your horse it will transfer to other animals as well. And the more you use it, the more natural it will become. Just as it happened instantaneously with Joe the crow, even without me consciously trying. It just was.

Here are a few exercises to help you send a message to your horse:

## HEART-TO-HEART COMMUNICATION

### Exercise #6 - Magnetic Hands

Have you ever held two magnets together and seen how they have a natural pull to be with each other if held the right way, and how if held the opposite way, they actually push each other apart?

Well this 'feel' is what we are looking for when we work with our own energy.

If you haven't done this with two magnets, try it first. I want you to feel what this is like, the natural pull and push.

Take two magnets and allow them to snap together naturally. Then turn one of the magnets round and try to put them together. You can't do it, can you? They won't allow you to put them together.

You will feel the energy between the two keeping them apart. Try this a few times so you can feel the energy that is keeping them apart. How does it feel? Can you see it? Is it thick or thin? Does it feel spongy?

So now that you know what that energy feels like, I want you to rub your hands together vigorously until they are warm. Then right after that, clap them 3 times.

Then I want you to start pulling and pushing your hands together, without touching them. Just as if you were playing with the two magnets again.

Do this quickly a few times until you can feel the same type of energy keeping your hands apart that you felt with the magnets. Keep your hands close to each other, but do not touch. You should be able to feel the energy pretty quickly.

See your hands as having opposite polarities just like the magnets. One hand has the north pole magnetic energy and the other hand has the south pole magnetic energy.

It should feel like there is something thick and spongy between your hands and an energy in both palms, a slight tingling. That is the trapped energy between your hands.

You can increase this energetic flow by moving your hands around in a small circular motion with your hands cupped, as if you were playing with a ball. You can play with the size of the ball and feel how the energy can get larger and smaller, thicker and thinner.

Practice this a few times when you're not with your horse and then once you can feel this energy well, do it when you are with your horse.

Then put both hands up towards your horse's nose. Let him look at and sniff both hands. Hopefully he will lick one of them. Let your horse choose which hand he licks to see which one he chooses.

If your horse licks your left hand, then it means that he is giving you his energy. If your horse licks your right hand, then it means that you are giving him your energy. It shows you how you are exchanging energy.

It also means that your horse can feel your energy and that the two of you are connecting heart-to-heart in that moment. Enjoy this exercise.

## Exercise #7 - Spot Visualization

Go to an arena with your horse and relax, hang out, find your center, and connect with your horse. Then I want you to close your eyes and visualize your horse walking over to a particular spot in the arena and standing there relaxing.

Put a picture in your mind, vividly, of your horse walking over to that one spot in the arena. You can also picture yourself in this visualization and how close or far away he is from you. Be very clear with your picture.

Bring the feelings of calm, relaxation, safety, and trust into your body and then picture all those feelings being in that one spot in the arena. The same place where you are visualizing your horse standing.

If you have a grass arena, picture your horse eating grass in that particular spot in the arena along with those wonderful feelings of security, trust, and calmness. Feel those feelings and thoughts in your own body too.

## HEART-TO-HEART COMMUNICATION

Send those feelings, thoughts, and/or pictures to your horse. It's like sending your horse a quick movie of him walking over and standing in that one spot. Along with the sounds and feelings that go along with that movie. You can do this with your eyes open or shut.

Play that movie in your head over and over until your horse hears you and agrees to go to that spot. Once your horse is there, you can go over and pet him and say thank you. After all, he not only heard you, but he also agreed to do as you asked.

You should know which type of communication is easier for you now. So go ahead and use that type of communication in this exercise. You can even try using a few of them if you really want to branch out and try something new.

But make sure your preferred method of communication works before you try a different one. You want to keep it simple and not make this too complicated. Complication may confuse you and your horse right now.

Make sure to think the thought clearly and picture where you want your horse to go. Be focused and use one thought at a time. Don't let your mind wander or change the location.

Remember to start small at first. Use small words, phrases, or thoughts. Use one emotion or feeling at a time. Use only one picture at a time. Then later you can experiment and try more.

I want you to start accepting and trusting your natural telepathic gifts and talents and believing in yourself.

Many people expect the floodgates to open up and in one instant as if they were hit by lightning, bringing with it a *"Eureka"* moment. But honestly, most of the time it shows up slowly in small moments. Little gems of connection that grow and accelerate over time.

You start to see and hear things, then you validate those as being real, then you get more comfortable listening and hearing more and more, then one day you realize it has become natural and it all comes together.

## SENDING A MESSAGE

But it takes time and practice, along with a lot of patience. I already believe that you can do this. Now you just need to believe in yourself.

You may feel that you're not getting a lot of information from your horse the first few times. You may also feel that because of this that you're not succeeding. But that's not the case. Even one thought, one feeling, one word is something to be excited about.

The more confidence you gain in yourself and your connection with your horse, the more it will come naturally.

Horses communicate simply. They don't have these long drawn-out conversations like humans do. They don't lie, they don't gossip, they don't get into the weeds about what's going on in their lives like humans do.

Your horse is not going to ask you what you did at work today or ask you about the latest gossip. Horses are also not going to try to fill up empty space or get nervous if both of you are silent. Horses are comfortable in silence. You need to be comfortable with silence as well. No pressure.

Horses will initiate a conversation when they have a need or they want to tell you something they feel is important.

One picture or image can tell a story that encompasses many words. One feeling can do the same thing. Be grateful for the simplicity of your horse's communication style and embrace it. Keep it simple.

You will eventually get it all. Just be happy with your connection and that things are starting to happen for you. How exciting is it to know that you are in the beginning of a transformation to a new way of communicating with your horse. And it only gets better from here.

**Results:**

Even though I talk about sending and hearing messages in this lesson, I want you to focus mainly on sending your messages.

Whether you hear something or not yet is not the point. The point

## HEART-TO-HEART COMMUNICATION

is that you practice sending your message. Just because you can't hear a response does not mean that you didn't send a message.

You should feel a stronger connection with your horse after this lesson. You should also feel more at ease with how you are sending messages. Practicing the steps over and over on how to send a message will make it easier the next time you try.

It's like learning to dance. At first you feel like you have two left feet and you're tripping over yourself all the time. But after you practice the steps over and over, your feet seem to know what to do without you having to think about it too much.

That's how I want you to be with sending messages. Just practice sending and sending and don't worry about the receiving until the next lesson.

# LISTENING & RECEIVING A MESSAGE

*"Messages from your horse can be as simple as saying 'I'm in pain' and then showing you where with a picture. They can also be as profound as this message a student received from her horse...*
*'I'm changing, you're changing, we are both being redirected, our souls are becoming one'."*
**Teddie Ziegler**

**Step #5 – Receiving Messages (Listening)**

Most people think of communicating as "talking" to someone. However, they forget the part about "listening" to someone. This is actually more important than the "talking" part.

Listening to your horse is a very important skill.

We humans are so used to talking all the time, it's easy for us. It's the listening part that is harder.

## HEART-TO-HEART COMMUNICATION

I'm sure you know lots of people that talk over others, cut others off in mid-sentence and start talking, and talk forever. These people are not good listeners. Conversations are made up of two parts – talking and listening.

I bet you talk with your horse all the time, verbally and non-verbally. However, you can't hear your horse yet. Maybe you can sometimes, but you're just not sure. But that's because you haven't learned how to listen to your horse's type of telepathic communication.

It's not that your horse isn't trying to talk with you, for the most part. It's that your internal listening skills need to be improved.

You can hear him when he calls your name through a whinny. Your ears can hear your horse's movements or when he's eating. And I bet you usually know where your horse is right before you see him.

But it's your heart that we are teaching to listen. And it's a heart-to-heart conversation that takes place silently, internally, and telepathically.

Please understand that your horse has an individual personality like anyone else and he may be more of a private, guarded, shy, or withdrawn horse. Which means he may take a while to talk with you. So, your horse may not talk with you until he has something important to share with you.

I have an autistic nephew who didn't speak for a number of years. But the first time he rode my horse Jazz, he said his first word, "Sweet". One word told me how wonderful he felt to be close to a horse and ride with me. He was in my lap on Jazz when he said it.

I know he and Jazz were having a conversation as he giggled and laughed while riding with me. Jazz seemed like he was laughing as well. They had an instant connection. It was beautiful to witness.

Doctors will say that sometimes an autistic child won't talk as early as other children because they just don't have anything they want to say. So if your horse isn't talking to you, maybe he just doesn't have anything he feels is important enough to share yet.

Then again, your horse may be more excitable, happy, and outgoing. Which means that he may be trying to send you lots of information and once you start talking, you're going to get an ear full.

If you are more of a visual person, you will probably receive messages from your horse as an image. If you are more of a physical person, then you may receive messages as a physical sensation.

If you are more of an emotional person, then you may receive your horse's message as a feeling. You may also receive a message from your horse as a simple knowingness or a thought.

However you receive your horse's message, acknowledge the response and say, "thank you for sharing with me". Even if you don't hear a response say, "thank you for your patience, I'm still trying to learn how to listen to you".

When receiving messages, sometimes people think that there is a right and a wrong answer. There isn't. There is just a response.

If you are looking for a "right" answer, you will shift into the logical side of your brain and get away from your emotional side. Therefore, cutting off your heart-to-heart connection because you stopped listening with your heart and started analyzing the answers.

Save that for later when you aren't with your horse. That's why I ask you to just write any responses you receive in your journal and look at them at a later date and in a different place, without your horse.

Later on, when you can understand these responses better and can communicate better, you will automatically know what the responses mean. It will be natural and a "gut feeling". You will understand without having to analyze or figure it out with your logical brain.

So, the first step in listening to your horse is to become calm, centered, and happy. The same thing you do when hanging out with your horse. And after you've sent your horse a simple, concise message through a thought, feeling, or a picture, then quiet your mind again.

After you have quieted your mind, allow yourself to open up. Open your heart, open your mind, and open yourself to hear your horse, internally. Open up and let go of any expectations and any judgements you may have.

Allow whatever your horse wants to send you to come through without trying to talk back or interpret the thought, feeling, or picture that you're receiving. But have your journal with you and write down whatever you're receiving.

Then afterwards tell your horse "thank you" and let him know that you really appreciate the conversation. Even if you didn't get anything, I'm sure he was trying to talk with you. So being appreciative of his effort will ensure that your horse keeps trying.

Every time you do this and all the exercises in this book, the better you will become, the easier the conversation will be, and the happier you both will be with your results.

I want you to feel comfortable with this form of communication and be confident about your skills. They are there and they will just increase with time and practice. Just keep practicing and don't give up.

Sometimes when people first start to hear their horse they doubt the process. They think they put the thought or image in their own head. Sometimes people think they imagined it. Sometimes they think they are just talking to themselves.

Don't doubt yourself. You will only stop the flow of communication and you will do the opposite of what this book is about. Trust in yourself as well as the process.

Trust the first response you sense, feel, or see without judgement or interpretation. You might not understand it right away, but you will with practice. Validate your own listening skills.

When learning to recognize and distinguish your own emotions from that of your horse, it is important to be receptive and validate whatever you receive. So when you do get images, emotions, or thoughts that you can say, "this could be from my horse", allow it to be from your horse.

Do not say it is your imagination, or that you're just talking to yourself. Believe in yourself and your horse.

If you are still doubting yourself, ask your horse a question that can be validated. Ask him something simple. This will help you learn to trust your listening skills.

If your horse is stressed, has some form of trauma, is in pain, or in fear, these can stop your horse from talking to you. His energy may be too low or too focused on other things to talk with you. Be compassionate for what your horse may be currently going through.

Be realistic with your expectations regarding your first attempts to communicate with your horse. It takes time to change your habits and the way you have been communicating with your horse for years.

However, the more time you put into doing these exercises, the more you will get out of this book. This in turn will help bring you and your horse closer and will make your heart-to-heart communication go smoother.

Here is an exercise to help you listen to your horse:

## Exercise #8 - The Art of Energy

I want you to tie your horse up in a quiet, peaceful location where he is happy and safe. Give him something good to eat that will take him about 10-15 minutes to finish. We want your horse happy and content standing in one place for a while.

Wherever you decide to tie up your horse, make sure it's a private place where you can practice this Reiki style exercise. You don't want any distractions or loud noises.

The first thing I want you to do is rub your hands vigorously and clap 3 times as you did in the "Magnetic Hands" exercise #6. Then do the

## HEART-TO-HEART COMMUNICATION

same push and pull with your hands until you can feel that thick, spongy energy again. Then I want you to get close to the side of your horse.

I want you to stand next to your horse without touching him, close your eyes, take 3 deep breaths in and out to relax and calm yourself.

I want you to get yourself in the right frame of mind to listen to your horse and help your horse clear any stress. This is a clearing exercise for your horse. It's a way to open up the lines of communication between the two of you and a way to make it easier for you to listen to your horse.

I also want your horse to know that you are setting yourself up to hear whatever he has to tell you and that you are open to anything he has to say.

Now open your eyes and keep your hands about an inch away from your horse's body. You should be able to feel the energy between your hands and your horse's body. If not, rub your hands together again and do the push and pull until you can feel it. Then hold your hands close to your horse again.

Then I want you to move your hands from the top of your horse to the bottom (no lower than his belly). Your hands should never actually touch your horse but be about an inch or so away from his body.

Then, with only your hands, start to brush away any negativity and resistance from your horse. Picture the negativity (or pain, or stress) leaving your horse's body and flowing away from both of you. Just like you would brush the dirt off your horse, you're brushing away stress.

Feel your horse calming down and relaxing as the issues are released and sent away from him.

Breath in and then out, releasing these things in yourself as well. Breathe in when you have your hands still and above your horse's body. Breath out when pulling out the stress and pushing it away.

This should open up a clear connection between the two of you as well.

When you feel it, connect, and tell your horse how much you love him. Send your horse your deep feelings of love and gratitude. This will reassure him and replace the negativity with positivity. Thereby instilling more trust and a willingness to talk with you.

Do this as long as the two of you are connected, relaxed, and happy. Don't forget to say, "thank you" when you're done.

After you are done, shake your hands towards the ground, away from your horse, releasing anything left over and any excess stress or energy.

Then just stand there next to your horse and touch him. Relax and connect with your horse again and just listen in silence.

See what feelings, thoughts, words, emotions, physical sensations, or pictures come to you. Let them come in and then let them go. Don't hold onto anything or try to interpret anything right now. Save that for later.

You are not sending your horse any messages in this exercise. You are only listening. While you are touching your horse, eyes closed, and listening, enjoy the connection.

Learning to listen is a huge step in communicating heart-to-heart. It is usually the hardest step as well and why I left it for last.

**That is the end of this exercise, but I want to address a few other things...**

You won't get through to your horse if you have any negative feelings or thoughts and the same goes for your horse.

Negativity is usually the biggest problem with listening because we all tend to over analyze or be over critical and negative with ourselves. So, ease up on yourself and your horse. It will make connecting to and communicating with your horse go much smoother.

Horses can say a lot with just one picture or one thought. They may be telling you a whole story in one picture. So don't worry if you get only one thought or one feeling. Be happy that your horse connected with you and allowed you to see something he wanted to show you.

Just let it come and go without judgement. Trying to over analyze will only stop the flow and break the line of communication. All that will come later. Just enjoy the fact that you are on the same wavelength for now.

Without judgement means that you don't interpret what or why you are getting these pictures or feelings. It also means don't judge yourself. Trust that what you are seeing and feeling are coming from your horse. Trust that you are listening to your horse.

Many times I've seen people judge themselves and think that they are putting thoughts and emotions into their own heads with their own feelings. This might be the case, but for now we don't care if it is or it isn't. You're getting these from somewhere and it's most likely coming from your horse.

It is common to want to interpret the responses you receive, especially if this is the first time you've received something. You may jump to conclusions based on your own experiences with your horse or by reading their body language. This is OK too.

As humans you may also tend to read too much into the responses you receive. This will balance itself out once you have more practice. So don't worry too much about this. Just listen to the words, thoughts, feelings, or images you receive.

You may not understand what you are receiving, but you will once you have more practice. For now, just release it and let it go. Don't judge. You can also write everything down in your journal and look at it later. It may not make sense today, but it might one week from now looking back.

Remember that once you stop to "figure out" what you are receiving, you actually stop the flow and stop any further communication. So, wait until after you feel your horse is done sending something to you and then write it down in your journal.

When your horse trusts you, he will talk with you. That's when he will feel he can share his thoughts and emotions with you.

# LISTENING & RECEIVING A MESSAGE

I want to clarify that when you are sending and receiving messages, sometimes you won't understand what you hear back. However, you don't have to at this point, just accept it. You are still in the beginning stages of your learning.

Here's an example of how beneficial Heart-to-Heart Communication can be:

> *I have 3 cats at my home in Maryland and all 3 of them were wild feral kittens that came into my life at the perfect times.*
>
> *Two of them, Wolfy and Toby, were kittens that their mother dropped off on my doorstep to take care of. They had health issues that are now fine, but their feral mother knew I'd take care of them.*
>
> *They were able to be inside/outside cats once their health issues were cleared up. Because of this they got to interact with their feral mother and siblings who lived under and on my front porch.*
>
> *They learned a lot from their mother on hunting, cleaning, and more importantly staying safe. There was a lot of wildlife at my home in California – raccoons, skunks, coyotes, dogs, hawks, possums, etc.*
>
> *But when we moved to Maryland there were new types of threats – people, cars, dogs, foxes, owls, etc. So I kept the two cats in all the time. They would sit by the open windows and watch, but they never seemed to want to venture outside either. I think they could feel the new dangers.*

# HEART-TO-HEART COMMUNICATION

*Then Tiger came into my life and their home. Tiger had been a feral barn cat that decided to come home with me. But that's an earlier story.*

*Even though Tiger had been an outside feral cat all her life, Tiger was very happy being an inside cat through the first winter with me. I think she was very grateful for the warmth and safety of a home, love, and lots of food.*

*But as soon as spring came around she wanted to go outside. I live in a housing development so it's very different from Tiger's 15-acre farm with lots of woodland around it.*

*I wasn't sure she would be safe so I held off letting her out. Then one day I realized she had gotten the other two cats involved and all 3 of them were at the front door wanting to go out.*

*So I decided to listen. But first I sat down with all 3 of them in their room and had a long talk with them about all the dangers in the area and what to watch out for. I showed them pictures of the dangers.*

*I also told them that I would make a deal with them. If they stayed on the front porch, or close by, and didn't run off I would let them out every day. But if they ran off, I would keep them in because I really didn't want to see anything bad happen to them. It would break my heart if I ever lost them.*

*We had all talked and they had agreed that if I let them out on their own for a few hours a day that they would stay on the porch or in the front garden where it is safe. And you know what? They have always done this for me.*

*For the entire last year that we have had this agreement in place, they have stayed right close to the house every day. And I can't tell you how wonderful it has been for all of us.*

*They get their time outside to enjoy the weather, watch the birds and butterflies, and smell all the other animals that have been around (I put out food for the neighborhood strays). They are very happy and they're safe.*

*And I'm happy because I know that they are safe and happy. It's a win-win.*

*That's how easy it can be when you can talk with your animals and have an actual conversation.*

**Results:**

The goal here in this step is to experience communication in a new way, heart-to-heart. However, this will not happen if you are feeling stupid, or timid, or scared. This will block your open heart.

You need to feel open and receptive to whatever happens and allow anything to happen. Listen completely.

**Trust and enjoy the process!**

# ALLOWING THE POSSIBILITIES

*"Take one thing at a time, one step at a time. Whatever you're working on…take a step back, look at the big picture, think about what you want to accomplish, and understand that there's always room to grow and be patient. Allow whatever is to happen and believe in the possibilities."*
**Teddie Ziegler**

## Step #6 – Allow, Rinse, and Repeat

Now that you have the whole process and have gone through it step by step, I want you to do it all over again, putting it together in your <u>own</u> way with your horse.

Allow whatever happens to happen, be grateful for it, and enjoy the entire process… both the good and the bad of it all.

Remember there is no right or wrong way – there is just your way.

Tweak what you need, keep what you want, discard what you don't want. But don't forget to listen with your heart.

This is a private and personal interaction and relationship with your horse. Learn to communicate by connecting the two of you heart-to-heart. Don't give up and stay as positive as possible.

It will work and you will succeed with time, patience, and love. I just know it!

<u>Here's one more story of how being able to communicate with your horse is so important:</u>

Every year in California there are wildfires. You can't always tell where they are going to crop up, but you do know that every year they will show up somewhere.

Well, one year I had my two horses, Jazz and Apollo, at a boarding facility in Willow Springs. It was a beautiful country area with hundreds of acres of woodlands. It was a great place to go on long trail rides through nature but it wasn't so great when a fire hit the area.

One day I was at home and all of sudden I just knew something was wrong because I could 'hear' my horses calling to me and I just knew I had to hook up the horse trailer and go. When I got closer I saw the smoke and flames coming down the hillside.

Trees, brush, and homes had caught on fire and with all the dry trees, the wildfire was spreading quickly and was headed for the boarding facility.

When I got there it was chaos. Other owners were already there along with some volunteers and they were all trying to get horses into trailers to get them out of the line of fire.

All the horses were panicking and the people there were panicking. It was really terrifying. I parked close to the pasture where Jazz and Apollo were along with 12-14 other horses.

## HEART-TO-HEART COMMUNICATION

The fire was getting so close by then that people were just opening the stall doors and pasture gates and letting the horses out because they had no other choice. There were more horses than there were trailers.

As I pulled up, somebody had just opened the pasture gate that I was close to and all the horses, including Jazz and Apollo, were running out as fast as they could away from the fire. I jumped out of my truck and shouted their names as loud as I could.

Fortunately they heard me and they immediately turned away from the herd and ran towards me. I opened up the back of the trailer and as they came galloping towards me, I thought… *"Get in and I'll get you to safety"*. They ran straight into the trailer and then looked back at me as if to say, *"Let's go, mom!"*.

I know how they felt and I wanted to get them out of there quickly, but there was so much mayhem with people and horses running everywhere that I felt I had to stop and help.

So I shut the doors to the trailer, told my horses that I would be right back, and ran over to another owner who was having trouble getting her horses loaded. I calmly told the horses, *"Get in, it's safer in there"*. The horses immediately got in and without looking round, I ran off to the next person to help. I only managed to help two other owners before the heat got too much and I could hear my horses calling to me.

I ran back to my trailer and shot off down the road. As I drove along, I could see all the loose horses running in all directions. So I told the horses to follow in the same direction as the cars as it would take them away from the fires to safety.

It was a nightmare and it happened so quickly. But fortunately all the horses survived and made it out safely even though the barn had burned to the ground and the facility was devastated.

Now you may think this all sounds a little too far-fetched but I'm just telling you what happened.

They say that preparation is everything, so wouldn't you want to be able to do the same with your horse if you were caught in a similar situation? Having a great relationship together on top of that then just becomes the most wonderful bonus.

# RESOLVING YOUR ROADBLOCKS

*"I will always be learning from my horses until the day I die because there's always something I can improve on and something new to learn."*
**Teddie Ziegler**

---

**What to do if you are hitting roadblocks:**

Most people struggle with their first few attempts to talk with their horse. I know because I struggled initially too.

I could feel some sort of connection with my horses and I could sometimes feel an emotion from them, but I couldn't regulate it. These feelings weren't consistent and that was about all I was able to achieve on my first few attempts.

If you are hitting roadblocks, below are some things I've learned along the way that have helped me. The most important thing to remember is… don't give up. Use some of these suggestions and try again. With patience, time, and practice, you can do this too.

# RESOLVING YOUR ROADBLOCKS

So let's start off by looking at some of the reasons you may be struggling:

- Your horse may be shy, closed off, or distrusting of humans.
- Your horse may not be ready or want to talk with you due to your current emotional state.
- Your horse may be trying to talk with you but you can't hear him.
- You may be too stressed, depressed, frustrated, or emotional to send or receive messages.
- You may be too needy and want it too much to allow it to happen naturally.
- Your mind may be too busy, you can't find stillness, and you can't stop thinking logically.
- You may feel nervous and anxious or you have performance fear that you will draw a blank.

Remember, you are learning a new language. The language of your horse, heart-to-heart communication. It takes time, dedication, and practice to get it right.

If you've ever tried to learn another language, think back to how long it took you to even begin to get good at it? How many hours a day were you in class with a teacher guiding you through your learning process?

Think of learning this skill in those terms and you'll make it much easier on yourself. Know that it is going to take a while and that it won't always go smoothly. That's OK, don't be hard on yourself. You won't get this overnight either but with desire, dedication, and guidance, you will get there.

It is natural to experience mental and/or emotional blocks when learning to communicate heart-to-heart. These are normal and happen to just about everyone when they first start out.

Here are some specific roadblocks and their solutions:

# HEART-TO-HEART COMMUNICATION

## Step #1 Roadblocks

If for some reason you are having trouble finding your center and quieting your mind, here are some other options that may help. You can try one of these or all of these.

Just find what helps you turn off your internal chatter and quiets your mind.

If you have too much internal chatter:

### Think One Thought:

- Sometimes giving your mind only one thing to focus on can help it quiet down. So when you are out with your horse hanging out and just enjoying nature, close your eyes and think of only one thing. Choose something very simple like the color BLUE.
- Picture the sky blue or whatever your favorite color of blue is. Focus on what that color looks like and allow it to take over your entire mind's view. Then think about how that color makes you feel. Feel that color within your body as you are seeing it in your mind.
- Then when you just can't hold that thought any longer let it go, open your eyes, and watch your horse for a while. Again, try not to think about anything other than how much you are enjoying watching what your horse is doing and being with him.
- Try to stay in the present moment and every time your mind starts to wander, go back to your one thought. Keep practicing this and it will begin to get easier each time.

### Be Realistic with Your Expectations:

- Be realistic about your goals and expectations. You may not be able to entirely quiet your mind and let go of all your thoughts. But at least you will be able to limit them and start the process.

- Accept the fact that your thoughts will come in and out sporadically and that's ok. Just acknowledge those thoughts and let them go. Don't give them any importance or judgement. Let them flow in and then out again, leaving your mind.

**Listen to the Sounds of Nature:**

- Sometimes it's easier to focus your mind on something you can hear. When you are hanging out with your horse you can try to listen to your surroundings while you have your eyes closed.
- Focus on the sound of the wind blowing through the tall grass, the trees and leaves rustling, the birds singing, the babbling of a nearby brook, and the sound of your horse eating. All of these sounds can help you find your center.
- This should stop your mind thinking of all the things you have to do, want to accomplish, or did yesterday and refocus it on the present moment again.

**Listen to Music:**

- Just like refocusing your brain, listening to nature, listening to calming music can also help quiet all those noisy thoughts in your head.
- Choose something calming and something that you really enjoy. It should be music that is soothing to your heart and mind. When I first started getting stuck with too many thoughts in my head, I listened to Music by Peter Kater. I especially enjoy his 'Element Series: Air'
- You can do this with your eyes open or shut. Whichever makes you feel more comfortable and relaxed.

### Breathing Exercise:

- If you are still having trouble trying to get yourself centered, calm, and happy let me give you one way that really helps me and is very quick and grounding… breathing.
- There are many different types of breathing exercises that can have physical effects on your body but this is the one that I use…
  - Find a quiet place to sit or stand before you get to your horse's stall or paddock.
  - Concentrate on your breathing and take a deep breath in and count to 4. Breathe deep and from the lower diaphragm. Breath in from your nose, mouth closed.
  - Hold the breath for a count of 5.
  - Then release the breath for a count of 6. Release the breath through your mouth.
  - Repeat this over and over until you start to feel calmer. Your breathing will become more controlled and slower when you have reached your goal.
  - Then think about a positive, peaceful, happy place or memory, smile and go see your horse.

## Step #2 Roadblocks

If for some reason you are having trouble opening your heart to your horse, here is another option that may help.

If you have trouble connecting to your horse:

### Ocean Visualization:

- When there are so many things going through your head that you can't really seem to connect with your horse and open your heart, I want you to visualize a large ocean.

## RESOLVING YOUR ROADBLOCKS

- Picture that this ocean is all encompassing and filling up your mind's view. Just like you pictured the word BLUE in the One Thought exercise above.
- Let all your thoughts, feelings, and whatever else is going on in your head float around in this vast ocean. Everything is in it. Picture all that 'stuff' as black words swimming, swirling around, or floating in this ocean.
- Then think about your horse and the fact that you truly want to connect and open your heart to him.
- Then as you are looking at that vast ocean filled with all the stuff in your head, realize that this ocean is blocking you from your horse and standing in your way. You can't even see your horse because of it. The ocean is your current block.
- Then picture the sun shining really bright and birds flying overhead and watch as your ocean begins to part. And all the stuff in your head either goes to the right or the left, along with the ocean waters.
- Picture this deep crevasse and the ocean parting in two. So that there is a dry, beautiful pathway that goes right through the middle of the ocean and it leads directly to your horse.
- Picture your horse on the other side of this pathway waiting for you and looking straight at you, wanting you to reach him.
- Then feel how this pathway is clear and safe. As you feel this, cross it to be with your horse and after you reach your horse let the water go back calmly. But remain with your horse, by his side, happy and safe.

This should help you connect with your horse by allowing you to visualize a pathway. This pathway is your heart-to-heart connection. Use this as often as you like.

HEART-TO-HEART COMMUNICATION

## Step #3 Roadblocks

If for some reason you are having trouble connecting to your horse, here are some options that may help.

When you first try this type of communication, you might want it so badly that you push yourself to get instant results. You want it to work overnight. Then when you can't, you feel bad, become over critical, and you close yourself off.

That is the exact opposite of what we are trying to accomplish in this program. This actually pushes your energy outward in judgement instead of inward with heart.

Have you ever tried to remember the name of something, on the spot, that you just can't quite get and the harder you try, the more you can't remember it?

But when you go to sleep or you're resting, all of a sudden the answer comes to your brain and you say, *"Aha, I remember!"*.

Your brain does the same thing when you are trying to push yourself too hard for instant results with this type of communication. Let it go. Go with the flow and the flow will get easier.

If you are trying too hard and looking for instant results:

### Relax:

- Go back to Exercise #3 and do the meditation exercise again until you're able to relax and let all the negative feelings go away. Even if it's only just for a few minutes. Then try to relax longer the next time you do it. You can listen to a meditation you do on your own or even relaxing music as above.
- There is no right or wrong in this entire program. You do you and follow the steps until you can figure out how your lines of communication with your horse can be achieved. For some people this process is quick and for others it takes longer.

# RESOLVING YOUR ROADBLOCKS

- It may also be your horse that is taking longer. There are two beings in this relationship and you both need to feel confident and comfortable with the process. Go slow. It's natural and OK to do so.

**The Name Game:**

- Because your mind can sometimes get stuck in a vicious cycle of self-criticism or putting too much pressure on yourself, here is a little trick I do to get myself unstuck. This might sound weird but it works every time for me.
- Choose one word that is simple and you can easily picture. I always start with the word TREE. This is a word association game.
- Now you are going to begin thinking of words that you can associate with that word. I want you to also say these words out loud to yourself. So the next word I think about could be leaves, or maybe green, or maybe Fall. There is no right or wrong answer.
- Then keep coming up with more words to associate until you get stuck or until you start laughing. That's what usually happens with me. And by the time that happens, I'm calm and happy. It works every time for me.
- After you've completed this you should have calmed down, or at least forgotten all the stuff that was causing the block. Basically, once you are happy with where you are and what you're doing, you will also enjoy being with your horse.
- For instance: My thoughts would go like this (and I picture the image in my head as I say each word out loud). Tree – leaf – green – blue – sky – clouds – painting – colors – crayons – children – Jacob – school – football – cleats – soccer – Eric – cats – rug – floors – hardwood - and on and on until my mind is settled and happy again. It might go on for 5-10 minutes. Whatever it takes to get unstuck.

## HEART-TO-HEART COMMUNICATION

- This can be quick or slow, whatever you feel comfortable with that makes you laugh.
- This quick Name Game exercise also gives you the ability to respond freely without a right or wrong answer and without judgement. This will get you talking, relaxed, and more vulnerable.

## Step #4 Roadblocks

If for some reason you are having trouble sending a message to your horse, here are some options that may help.

If you are doubting yourself:

**Go Back:**

- Go back to Exercise #7 and do the Spot Visualization exercise again as well.
- After doing this again, it should open you up and your heart for a clear line of communication.
- Doing the Spot Visualization will also help validate that you are sending messages to your horse and that he is listening to you. You don't need to hear him say anything. You just want him to go to the spot that you are visualizing.
- Make sure the spot you want him to go is someplace safe, comfortable and somewhere that he is used to going. Do what's easy first and as you get better at this you can progress further.

**Practice:**

- Pay attention to what you're sending. You're working on the foundation of your communication with your horse and building it from the ground up. Your communication will grow and become clearer with patience and practice.

# RESOLVING YOUR ROADBLOCKS

- Don't doubt and don't compare yourself to others. You have your own style and so does your horse. You just have to figure out what that style is. But once you start to learn what this is, embrace it and be grateful that you have started to learn how to communicate heart-to-heart.

**Photograph:**

- To help you stay connected to your horse and practice your stillness, have a picture of your horse with you as often as you can. This can be a picture on your phone, but a real photograph is even better. A tactile response is better to help connect the two of you.
- Then when you are somewhere where you feel calm or your mind is quiet for a short time, pull out the photo and look at it. Imagine how wonderful you feel and how much you love your horse and send those good feelings to your horse through the picture. Just send your loving feelings, thoughts, and maybe even a picture of the last time you both were together having fun.
- That's it. Just do this whenever you can. This will help you connect even deeper with your horse when the two of you are together and this will help you communicate more freely as well. Your horse will hear your messages of love every time you look at that photo.

Almost everyone doubts what they are sending or receiving. It's normal. You need to accept your own validation and feel good about your progress. Even one word, one thought, one feeling is good.

Be patient with yourself and your horse. Heart-to-Heart communication is meant to be natural and non-stressful. This is not supposed to be intimidating or adding pressure to you

HEART-TO-HEART COMMUNICATION

or your horse. But you will have your ups and downs as with learning anything new.

Communication can be simple and because of this people often don't trust what they are sending or receiving. They think it's too easy, there must be something wrong. Don't let that be you. Enjoy the process and relax. It is already happening, whether you know it or not.

## Step #5 Roadblocks

If for some reason you are having trouble receiving a message from your horse, or listening, here are some options that may help.

If you think that you're projecting your feelings and thoughts onto your horse:

### Validate:

- Go back and do Exercise #4 Describe your Horse again. Close your eyes and do this until you can describe every part of your horse. You should be focused on picturing every piece in your head. It will work like the Name Game did to get you out of the judgement zone.
- Then go one step further and start asking yourself how your horse is feeling at this moment. Keep your eyes closed when you ask yourself. Then open your eyes and look at your horse to validate what you are feeling. Keep doing this until you feel more comfortable validating your own feelings.

### Be Confident:

- Feel confident that whether you are or whether you're not projecting your feelings onto your horse, it doesn't matter. If

# RESOLVING YOUR ROADBLOCKS

you feel any feelings at all, they are coming from your horse. Your horse has to be sending these to you. So if you are seeing these or feeling these in yourself, believe that your horse put them there.
- Sometimes it seems too easy. Let it be easy. You may feel certain things because of what you know or what you see in your horse's body language. That's OK. That goes back to being able to validate your thoughts and feelings. But you can still trust your feelings.
- The exercises in this book give you the opportunity to experience your horse's perceptions rather than staying stuck in your own. You can see things through your horse's eyes, feel things through his body, and think thoughts that come from his mind.
- Accept and allow all of it to happen. You will get better at discernment as you practice.

As this book now comes to a close, I thought it was only appropriate to remind you that everything can be improved. Always.

It doesn't matter if you're trying to improve something at work, at home, or you are trying to improve your relationship with your horse, there is always room for further improvement.

I will always be learning from my horses until the day I die because there's always something I can improve on and something new to learn. I look forward to continual growth and adventures with my horses.

Take one day at a time, one step at a time. Whatever you are trying to improve, take a moment to take a step back mentally, look at where there is room to grow and then just figure out how to do it. Trial and error is an acceptable way to learn.

But don't expect to solve everything at once. Chunk your learning down into smaller sections. This makes whatever you are trying to do or improve go smoother, and it's also easier to work in baby steps. So if you need to break one of the exercises into smaller chunks, don't be afraid to do it.

# HEART-TO-HEART COMMUNICATION

**As I always say, *"Push the easy button whenever possible".***

And remember, whether that baby step worked for you or not, it is still a step in the right direction. You've learned something from it. Even a so-called 'failure' will teach you how to do it better next time. So try again but tweak it. And then keep going. Every lesson is an opportunity for improvement.

It is all in how you look at the situation. Perception is important. So keep it positive and you will continue growing and improving. I wish you all the best and all my heart-felt wishes that you do indeed realize the dreams you hold for you and your horse.

I trust and know that the two of you will have some wonderful conversations in the future, and I too will feel blessed knowing that I helped you find such happiness. Have an amazing time learning and growing together! And drop me a line sometime to let me know how it's going.

# THE KIND OF RESULTS YOU CAN EXPECT

*"When you can deliberately tap into this energy
and hone this skill, a mere twitch of your head
or a shift in your seat is enough for your horse
to know exactly what you're asking.
And the two of you will be in perfect sync."*
**Teddie Ziegler**

<u>Here is a story one of my students sent me about an experience she had:</u>

"Last winter during the Holiday season, I went to see Choupette as she is outside 24/7. But when I got there to take her for a walk, she did not want to come out of her pasture.

It wasn't because she did not want to be with me as she stood next to my shoulder quite happily. But every time I tried to *put her halter on she would move her head away or cross her front foot over.*

*We all know how difficult it can be to halter a horse who does not want to be haltered. I didn't understand what was going on. What had I done wrong, I wondered?*

*That night back at home, I asked her in my mind what was happening so that I could understand. What I got from her was an image of a big black, loud monster moving very fast.*

*I didn't know what it meant but I immediately told her I understood her fears, that I was going to protect her, and that she would always be safe with me. I sent her visualizations of me haltering her and going out of her paddock.*

*And the next time I went to see her, that is exactly what happened. She came right to me and put her head in the halter and out we went without any problem.*

*A few days later I met another boarder and she told me that snowmobiles had been coming from the top of the hills down to the pastures, very close to the fences. These were ridden by men in black suits and helmets.*

*Choupette was telling me that she did not want to go out away from the safety of her pasture because of these snowmobiles. She was not being fussy, she had real concerns."*

<u>Earlier in the book I introduced you to my Uncle David and I thought you might like to hear another story about him…</u>

# THE KIND OF RESULTS YOU CAN EXPECT

When I got married, Uncle David came to the ceremony. Before I went into the church he came over to me and we chatted a little and then he asked me about the weather. I thought it an odd question and just said that I hoped it wouldn't rain given all the dark clouds overhead.

To which Uncle David jokingly said, *"I'll see what I can do about the weather for you."* We laughed and then I went into the church to get married.

When we came out of the church the sky was bright blue and the sun was shining! I was of course delighted that my big day just got a whole lot better.

But towards the end of the reception, Uncle David came to me and said that he had done his best to hold off the weather but maybe it was time to take the reception inside.

It was still clear blue skies when he said this and naturally, the guests thought we were nuts to be all heading back inside when it was still sunny.

So you can imagine their surprise when 15 minutes later it quickly got dark and then suddenly started pouring down rain.

Everyone asked me how Uncle David knew. I just looked over at him and smiled, "He just does" was all I could say.

Uncle David could not only tap into this universal energy I discussed earlier, but it naturally flowed through him. He could do and see things that other people couldn't even imagine. He could see a person's aura and tell you things about yourself that would blow your mind.

I instinctively knew to trust Uncle David and I took everything he said as gospel truth. At the time I couldn't explain it, but I knew to trust him. I knew he was connected to something I couldn't see and he was listening to something I couldn't hear. At least not at that time in my life.

I didn't think about it at the time but looking back, I guess I always did things a bit differently too, like sharing a two-way communication with animals. We just seemed to understand each other instinctually and naturally.

## HEART-TO-HEART COMMUNICATION

Being sensitive and being able to tap into that universal energy, to listen to it, to hear it, and to use it to talk to your horse is the secret to a truly magical relationship with horses because they are also a part of the universal energy.

That's what it's like for me and I absolutely know this is why horses are drawn to me and why people look at what I can do with them as miraculous.

It's also why I am able to work with hard-to-handle, shut down, and last-chance horses. The more shut down they are, the happier they are to see me. They are so excited to tell me what's been going on and have someone listen to them on their terms.

These horses know that I am connected to the same universal energy that they are and they instantly trust me. They want to be with me, talk to me, and interact with me.

I was blessed to be able to learn from Uncle David before he passed on and since then I've been able to not only hone this skill but work out how to pass this gift on to others.

I believe this is a natural ability we all have. We just have to be aware of and be open to connecting and learning how to tap into this energy and listen. Talking to your horse in a deeper, richer way is a part of this.

The ability to tap into this energy allows you to step into your horse's world simply, easily, and effortlessly. That has been my secret as to how I get the cooperation and love from my horses to fulfill my wildest dreams.

And the best news is that you can do all those amazing things with your horse too. Let this book be your guide to help you connect to your horse and tap into the universal energy.

Everything is possible if you believe. If you can gain this spark and develop a connection to this energy, it will all fall into place for you and your horse as well.

# THE MISSING INGREDIENT

*"For each horse I have owned, there was one
moment when I felt them connect. When we fell IN
LOVE and our relationship became different."*
**Teddie Ziegler**

Before I leave you, I want to tell you one more story:

I got a shock last week and it really affected me for some reason.

One of my friends that I play pool with every week told me that his wife had left him after 27 years. He said that she came home and said, *"I love you but I'm not IN LOVE with you anymore."* Then she walked out, moved in with a friend and just like that, it was over.

He was shocked and couldn't even fathom what it all meant. They were friends even before they married. They have two children, one in High School and one in College. Plus they had just got back from a lovely surprise trip that he arranged for their wedding anniversary.

He said they had laughed, had fun, and everything seemed normal,

## HEART-TO-HEART COMMUNICATION

he had no idea there was a problem. He has been happy for years and thought she was too. He wishes there had been some clues so he could have tried to talk the issues out and fix them.

**He says there is nothing more important to him than his family.**

This whole breakup thing shook me. I always looked at their marriage as being as solid as a rock. He has always been devoted to her, smiles when he talks about her, never complains, puts up with anything she does, takes care of her, and is a true gentle heart.

She is vibrant, rambunctious, funny, energetic (and a bit high-maintenance). But she always looked happy and was always smiling and joking around. The whole thing didn't make any sense to me, which is why it came as such a shock.

How could the relationship between two people who looked so much in love and happy, come to such a jarring and sudden end?

Apparently, his wife won't talk about it, doesn't want to work it out, and won't even take his calls. And all he wants is to have her back and he says he'd do anything to have her back, make it work, and make her happy. Despite the slap in the face he's had, he's still all pure love and devotion.

What I saw in his eyes and felt in his heart was the same dedication and desire that I had to find Apollo when he was stolen from me.

If you haven't read that story, you will find it here…

https://teddiezieglerhorsemanship.com/apollos-return/

I recognized the same emotion in my friend. He was determined and IN LOVE with his wife.

**Then those words kept repeating in my head *"I love you but I'm not IN LOVE with you".***

It's really hard to explain the difference, but I totally understand what she was saying. I had two male friends and after years of being just friends both of them proposed to me at different times. I used that same line with them.

I loved them as friends and would do almost anything for them if they ever needed me. But I didn't feel that deep, heart pounding, true love that made my heart sing every time I saw them. Do you know what I mean?

When I met my husband I knew right away there was something different about him, about us. I felt happy but at a completely different level than with a friend. It's hard to explain but if you've been fortunate enough to experience it, you'll know exactly what I'm talking about.

That spark, that light, that true heart-felt joy is what brought my husband and I together. It is also what keeps us together through the ups and downs of life. I can't imagine going through this life without him by my side. However, before I met him… I thought I didn't need anyone.

Before I met him, I was happy. I had a good life, good friends, and a great family. I enjoyed my career and my life. But now, that heart-felt joy in me has increased to another level that I didn't even know existed and could never have imagined.

Just as there was a moment in time when I could pinpoint a dramatic increase in love and joy when I met my husband… there was also a moment in time when I could pinpoint a dramatic increase in love and joy with my horses. I'll never forget that moment when I truly felt connected with Jazz. And another moment when Apollo and I connected that deeply.

For each horse I have owned, there was one moment when I felt them connect. When we fell IN LOVE and our relationship became different. There really is an AHA moment. When I felt it with Jazz for the first time it was so powerful that I just broke down and cried. I was so shocked.

Thinking about what happened with my friends brought me back to thinking about those incredible moments in my life when I truly connected deeply to my horses and them to me. I cherish those moments.

That deep connection, both human and horse being IN LOVE. That is the main component missing from most partnerships.

I believe it is also the missing component in almost all of the training programs that I have seen through the years.

Yes, I know you can't train someone how to fall IN LOVE with their horse and vice versa. But I can teach you the steps to a better relationship which then brings you the closeness and the ability to fall IN LOVE with each other. I bring you the opportunities to fall in love.

One of my students told me this after completing my personal coaching program:

> *"One thing for sure… I know she loves me
> and I know she knows I love her"*

You would not believe how big a step that was from where they started. She had always loved her horse and had done everything she could to make her happy but nothing worked. What made it even more painful was that she knew that her horse didn't really like her. So sad.

She told me she could sense there was a component missing but could never find it. Now that she has, they are IN LOVE and their partnership is incredible. She has the horse of her dreams and her horse has the human of her dreams.

Just like a marriage, you need to continuously work on it and keep the spark alive. Just because you were IN LOVE once, doesn't mean it's going to always be the same. Just as I saw with my friends who have been married for 27 years.

I am always telling my husband that we need to do things together to stay connected and sometimes we may need to re-connect. Weekly date nights, surprise adventures, flowers or cards, and maybe even a poem if it comes from the heart.

And it's not about the getting. It's about the giving.

Give what you feel in your heart, give what you want to see in your partner, give without any expectations of a return. Don't ever take being in love for granted. And the magic will happen for you too. This works for your human partner as well as your horse partner.

Fall IN LOVE all over again and watch how everything becomes simpler and easier with your horse and with your training. Add play dates, treats just to show your love, hugs and scratches filled with emotion, and just hang out together for hours doing nothing but enjoying each other's company.

Add those things to your current routine and you'll see the magic start to happen. Enjoy and be happy. I hope your horse makes your heart sing with true love and joy and vice versa.

# WHAT TO DO NEXT?

*"Everything is still possible, even if you don't believe it right now."*
**Teddie Ziegler**

I hope this book will help you and your horse on your way to an incredible, loving, and rewarding relationship together that lasts a lifetime.

**Most of my clients are horse enthusiasts who:**

- Are new to horses and need help with the fundamentals and want to start off at liberty.
- Have a brand-new horse that isn't like any other horse they've ever owned and they can't quite figure him/her out.
- Know they are missing some pieces of the horse jigsaw puzzle and neither they, the programs they've bought, nor the trainers they've hired have been able to find them.

# WHAT TO DO NEXT?

- Or know they are missing that special component that makes the difference between having a functional relationship and actually being IN LOVE with each other.

If you find yourself in any of these situations, here's how I can help.

I have a series of inexpensive programs to get you started and give you a flavor of my approach.

<u>7-Day Quick Start Program</u> – This course is designed to kick-start your confidence. Whether you've lost it completely or are just feeling unsure around horses, then this is the perfect primer to get you back on track.

<u>Foundation of Trust</u> – Start to gain the trust of your horse again or for the very first time. Learn to start trusting your horse again. Watch how approaching horses with a completely new mindset will transform your views on how horses operate. Learn to see the world through your horse's eyes and turn the world upside down to find solutions.

<u>Teddie's Fundamentals</u> - A common problem I see is the use of outdated, basic handling skills which ignore the needs of the horse and destroy any hope of a real relationship. Learn how I do the basics and how these fundamentals of horsemanship can help you too.

<u>Equine Qi Gong</u> - If you're stressed and anxious around your horse, this is the perfect way to relax, take your mind off your problems, and focus on the positive energies around you with the help of a true Qi Gong Master.

<u>Beginning The Connection</u> - Watch the journey as I take a complete novice, who knows nothing about horses and is even afraid of them, and transform him into someone who is confident and comfortable around horses. It will give you a sneak peek into how you can begin growing a deeper bond with your horse as well.

<u>The Stallion Series</u> - In this documentary-style video series, you will learn how easy and effective compassionate horse training can be as you

## HEART-TO-HEART COMMUNICATION

watch me take two Arabian Stallions from ignored and unpredictable to happy and trusting. A masterclass in patience and love.

I also offer a series of small group coaching programs, which are ideal if you are looking for a more personal learning environment with direct access to me but don't need the full 'hands-on' experience of being a personal coaching client.

Here's a quick overview of the process we go through when you become a personal client:

1. The first thing we do is get you to learn how to start over and hit the reset button to give your brain and your horse a rest. Time to shake off the issues, the problems, the should-haves and the could-haves, and clean the slate. I teach you how to get out of the *"I can't"* and say, *"I can,"* and mean it.

2. The second thing that we do is teach you how to rebuild from nothing. I help you put the building blocks that you know, along with a few new ones, in the right place and in the right order to build a strong, trusting, and confident foundation that can withstand the test of time.

   We work directly together to personally "audit" what's working and what's not, in order to develop an easy-to-follow plan of action specifically designed for your needs and your horse.

3. The next step in the process is to work together one-to-one on a weekly basis to fine-tune your individualized training program. This allows immediate help to correct issues and fine-tune results right away. You have direct access to me personally to resolve any issues or questions instantly as well.

## WHAT TO DO NEXT?

There's no waiting until next week or next month to find out how to fix a current issue. No remembering a question you have or trying to remember how your horse responded a week ago. You can text me immediately, and I respond right away. Or we set up a phone call the same day to talk it through. And you get to talk to me directly, not a student of mine or a student of a student.

The fine-tuning is done immediately, and this resolves further problems that could occur if you have to wait too long for an answer. As a result, progress happens more quickly and easily because of this special access and fine-tuning.

4. The last step is to walk you through a proven easy-to-follow method, a blueprint, supporting you the entire time. We go through each step together and individualize the results for your needs and that of your horse. No matter what personality, what issues, or the breed or age of the horse, we make it work for the betterment of your horse.

    I tailor the program to you and your horse to specifically address your hopes and dreams, as well as solutions to the challenges you are experiencing and your horse's core issues. This is a very personalized process to make sure that you get exactly the results you want, and I stick with you until you do.

Not only do you get access to the actual person who developed the program and who helps you along your path, but you also get someone who loves your horse almost as much as you do and someone who cares about your goals and progress and won't give up on you.

I love teaching and sharing everything I know so that my students can do exactly what I do. I teach you how to hone your instincts and become a natural horseman or woman in your own right.

## HEART-TO-HEART COMMUNICATION

Through the coaching, you will learn not only how to fix any current issues, but any and all future ones will just melt away due to the strength of the foundation you and your horse will build together.

Horses have this uncanny knack of pinpointing our weaknesses. When we can't get them to do what we want, it leads to frustration and disappointment as we lose our confidence. Soon enough, we give up all hope of realizing our dreams, and we tolerate a less than perfect partnership with our horse.

Don't let that happen to you. Everything is still possible, even if you don't believe it right now. So many times, clients have told me they'd resigned themselves to living with their issues, and then within months of working with me their horse is hanging on their every word and genuinely wants to be with them.

That can happen to you, too, so book a complimentary call, and let's see what we can achieve together: https://teddiezieglerhorsemanship.com/book-call/

My ultimate goal is to make you as self-sufficient as possible to the point that I become the last trainer you'll ever need to go to or study with. I want to teach you how to do it all yourself and learn how to continue achieving your dreams.

When I tell this to business people, they always tell me it's not a very good business model, but I don't care.

To me, it's like the story of the Wall Street banker telling the fisherman from the Caribbean how together they can build a massive fish empire that will make them so rich that they can retire to a tropical island, hang out with their buddies, drink beer and go fishing…

As Uncle David told me, this is what I am here to do. This is my gift, my life's work.

Dreams do come true, so never give up.

I wish you and your horse all the love and success in fulfilling your goals!

# DEDICATION

I want to take this last section just to say thank you to all the wonderful horses I have shared my life with. They have been such a blessing, taught me so much and shown me so much love, I Will be forever grateful to all of them.

Special thanks to my feisty and brave Quarter-Horse Paint, Jazz, who was with me for 34 years.

And to my other horses…

Special thanks to Jazz's son, Apollo, my smart and gentle Quarter-Horse, who was with me for 31 years.

Special thanks to my compassionate and loving Andalusian, D'Artagnan, who passed away too young and was only with me for 9 years.

# DEDICATION

And special thanks to my new little one that is not so little anymore, Merlin. My beautiful and courageous Friesian, who is only a year and a half old at this point and 16.3hh.

This picture is when we first met, at 5 months old, and I told him he was coming home with me.

Printed by Libri Plureos GmbH in Hamburg, Germany